PUBS OF THE RIVER THAMES

*This book is dedicated to my wife Rose,
for her love, inspiration and support
throughout our life together.*

Acknowledgements

*I would like to offer my sincere thanks to the following for their help
and encouragement, without whom this book would not have been
possible. To my mother, whose knowledge of history proved invaluable
and also her assistance in checking my manuscript. To my family for
the sacrifices they made so I could concentrate all my time and effort
on the book. To all the landlords, landladies, managers and staff of
the pubs who gave up their valuable time to answer my questions
and to those who provided me with a cup of coffee when needed. To
the librarians in the numerous libraries that I visited, whose help
and knowledge proved invaluable. Finally, thanks to my publishers,
for having so much faith in my idea and for all their help in
producing this work.*

Author's notes

*All the photographs for this book were taken on what I consider one
of the best manual medium-format cameras ever produced, the
Pentax 67. The two lenses used were a wide angle 45mm and a
standard 105mm (equivalent to 24mm and 50mm lenses on a
35mm system). Lighting on the internal shots was by means of
several Photax 500 watt tungsten heads and the filmstock used was
tungsten balanced Fujichrome 64T. For the exterior shots, I used
Fujichrome Velvia rated at the lower speed of ISO32, which I have
found gives the best results.*

PUBS OF THE
RIVER THAMES

MARK TURNER

Published in 2000 in Great Britain by
Prion Books Limited, Imperial Works, Perren Street,
London NW5 3ED

A catalogue record for this book is available from
the British Library.

ISBN 1-85375-349-1

Printed in Singapore by Kyodo

CONTENTS

RIVERSIDE INNS

'Every drop of the Thames is liquid 'istory.'
John Burns, 1858-1943

From its official source at Kemble in Gloucestershire to
the Thames Barrier at Woolwich in south-east London, the
course of the River Thames meanders through an
ever-changing landscape.

Above The Head of the River, Oxford

6

Starting from what is now normally a dry field, this increasing vein of water flows through sedate countryside, small villages, towns and cities to its final destination, the North Sea.

In Roman times, the Thames became one of England's most important waterways. Without it, the metropolis of Londinium, as it was then known, may not have been created. For a time it was possible to travel from the Bristol Channel to the Thames estuary by means of two rivers and a canal, but with the advent of the railways and steam power, the river became virtually redundant, apart from the main London ports.

Following the cessation of industrial river traffic, the idea of a Thames Path to provide public access was first debated over a hundred years ago. It is now possible to walk from the source to the Thames Barrier.

All along the river are examples of that great British institution – the public house. Throughout this book, you will find country inns, thatched taverns and village and city pubs, each with its own background and history.

Over the last few years, opening hours have become more flexible and you will now find the vast majority of pubs stay open all day, especially in summer. Some may close during the afternoon, particularly in winter or when it is quiet, but most landlords will try to accommodate everyone's needs if they are asked beforehand.

Virtually all the pubs in this book serve real cask-conditioned beer. Try some of the different styles available such as best bitter, golden beer, stout, porter or Indian pale ale. A wonderful assortment of food is also on offer, from filled rolls at the smaller pubs to three course meals.

Since I began this book, there have of course been changes in ownership of some breweries and pubs. Fortunately, most of the hostelries have been established long enough for them to have retained their unique character despite many comings and goings over the years.

I hope you enjoy visiting the pubs in this book. They are a part of British heritage, and must be preserved at all costs. Remember, if we do not use them, we will lose them, and once gone they will never return.

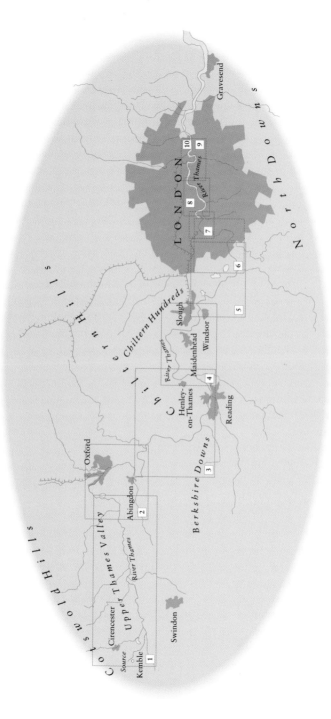

Above Map showing the route of the Thames and the areas covered by each chapter

KEY TO SYMBOLS

pub opening hours: may be subject to change or have seasonal variations.

cask-conditioned beers: range of cask beers (real-ale) served either by handpump or gravity.

Food serving times: Ⓥ vegetarian options available.

car park: the pub has its own free parking facilities, which may range from a few spaces to a large parking area.

garden/patio/terrace: outside area for drinking and eating products bought on the premises. Facilities may range from a few tables outside to a large garden with children's play area and barbecue.

children welcome: well-behaved children supervised by an adult allowed in certain areas of the pub.

dogs welcome: dogs allowed in certain areas of the bar or gardens, if supervised and kept on a lead at all times.

real fires: provision of coal or log-burning real fire. These will be lit at the discretion of the landlord.

no smoking area: a no-smoking area provided in the bar or dining area. Some pubs provide ventilation and smoke extraction facilities.

accommodation: facilities and prices for rooms may differ so please telephone the establishment for further details. No assessment of the rooms has been made by the author.

traditional pub games: these may include darts, bar billiards, aunt sally (players throw sticks or balls at a wooden dummy), boules, shove ha'penny, cards and dominoes.

moorings: riverside pubs where moorings are provided for customers.

NOTE

All opening and food serving times have been provided by each establishment, but these may be subject to change. It is advisable to ring before making your visit.

While credit cards are accepted in the vast majority of pubs, there are still a few that do not, and some also refuse to accept charge cards.

KEMBLE
TO
APPLETON

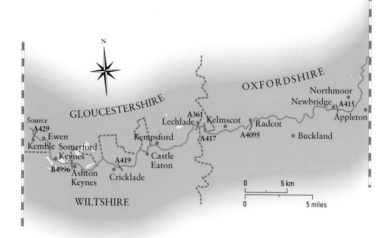

In the middle of a nondescript field called Trewsbury Mead,
near the village of Kemble in Gloucestershire, lies what is
widely accepted as the source of the River Thames, though it is
now dry for most of the year.

The site is marked by a simple stone. The grand statue of Old Father Thames, which guarded the spot for over sixteen years, was moved to St John's Lock at nearby Lechlade in 1974. The new stone is sheltered by an ash tree, reputed to be over two hundred years old and appropriately its trunk is engraved with the initials TH, which most people assume stands for Thames Head, though it could be only the initials of a courting couple.

A little distance from here running water appears. The first village on its route is Ewen, which means the source of a spring, and there are other contested sources of the Thames close by. Mill Farm is where the first mill on the Thames once stood, though it is difficult to believe that the young and developing river had enough power to turn a watermill. Running on, ever expanding, the river flows through Somerford Keynes with some evidence of old water mills, originally used for grinding corn. The Keynes part of the village name comes from its former owners, a dominant Norman family.

The Thames now leaves Gloucestershire and enters Wiltshire. The series of small bridges across the river at Ashton Keynes allow the local householders access to their Cotswold stone dwellings without getting their feet wet. Within the village are four stone crosses that were once used for mediaeval preaching.

Next is the market town of Cricklade, which in the 11th century had its own mint and reputedly had a castle at some time, although there are no signs of this now. In 1016, King Canute and his armies came through Cricklade, raiding their way to the Midlands. The first pub that is actually on the riverbank is at the small village of Castle Eaton. It is possible to cross the river here by means of the iron bridge that replaced an earlier stone crossing.

Now returning into Gloucestershire, the Thames soon reaches Kempsford, where the old ford was an important feature in mediaeval times. John of Gaunt, fourth son of Edward III and at one time head of government, had an estate here and the ghost of his sister-in-law, Lady Maud, is still reputed to walk the Thames path at night.

The navigable Thames starts just south of Lechlade at Inglesham. At this point the now disused Thames and Severn Canal joined the river to allow the barges access to the towns and villages along the route and eventually the great Port of London. Lechlade itself was once an important and busy market town because of the river: some of the stone used to build St Paul's Cathedral was mined nearby and carried from here. At Kelmscot the great Manor House still stands. It was once the summer house of the artist, interior decorator, poet, writer and printer William Morris.

Continuing eastwards through idyllic countryside, the Thames reaches Radcot where the 13th-century bridge across the water is the oldest on the river. It has been the scene of many battles over the years and has suffered much damage as a result, though fortunately the stone used to build and repair it came from Taynton quarry, just 10 miles away.

The river's next encounter with a road is at Tadpole Bridge, which was built at the end of the 18th century. The Thames then enters the small hamlet of Newbridge, where there is a pub at each end of the bridge even though there are no houses in the vicinity. The river soon turns northwards to flow past the marshland village of Northmoor. The marriage of Betty Rudge, a ferryman's daughter, and Lord Ashbrook took place in its 13th-century church, an alliance that because of the class system was considered totally unacceptable at the time.

Across the water lies the village of Appleton, very much an area where the majority of locals have moved away and a growing army of 'weekend' home-owners now inhabits the thatched cottages. The 12th-century Appleton Manor still remains.

Opposite The Rose Revived, Newbridge

THE THAMES HEAD INN

TETBURY ROAD, KEMBLE, NR CIRENCESTER, GLOUCESTERSHIRE

The Thames Head Inn, renamed due to its proximity to the great river's source, was at one time more under the influence of the Swindon to Gloucester railway line which runs behind the pub. It started life during the latter part of the 19th century as the Railway Hotel, in a building thought to have been constructed for the engineers working on the new branch line which opened in the mid 1840s. It kept this name until 1923, when it was changed to the Great Western.

Around 1992 it was changed to its present title, as by then the Thames Path had been firmly established. In fact it is possible to walk from the car park of the pub to the source without having to encounter the traffic on the main Cirencester to Tetbury road.

11.00-3.00, 6.00-11.00 Mon-Sat; 12.00-3.00, 7.00-10.30 Sun.

Arkell's 2B & 3B. Cider: Strongbow.

11.00-2.30, 6.00-10.00 Mon-Sat; 12.00-2.30, 7.00-10.00 Sun. ⓥ

SYMBOLS: 🅿 ❄ 👫 🏠 ♿ ✂ 🚮 🛏

TEL: *01285 770259*

WILD DUCK INN
DRAKES ISLAND, EWEN, NR CIRENCESTER, GLOUCESTERSHIRE

Situated in a quiet village in the Gloucestershire countryside, this converted barn dating back to 1563 is built from Cotswold stone, which radiates a brilliant golden yellow colour in the sunlight. Its unimposing exterior hides its identity as a superb inn. The olde worlde décor, inglenook fireplace, antique furniture and candlelit tables – and the ghost – all serve to take you away from 20th-century civilisation.

A past customer, Cornelius Uzzle, would wait until the bar was full and then devour 12 pounds of raw bacon. Afterwards he would pass round his hat to reap the rewards for his efforts. While gammon may still be on the menu, there is a good variety of other dishes, all cooked to order, including a wide selection of fresh fish. The Duck Pond Bitter, brewed especially for the pub by a secret brewery, is worth trying.

11.00-11.00 Mon-Sat; 12.00-10.30 Sun.

Courage Directors, Duck Pond Bitter (house beer), Smiles Best, Theakston XB, Theakston Old Peculier. Cider: Strongbow.

12.00-2.00 Mon-Sun, 6.45-10.00 Mon-Sat, 7.00-9.45 Sun. ⓥ

SYMBOLS: 🅿 ❄ 👫 🏠 ♿ 🚮 🛏

TEL: *01285 770310*

-FRESH FISH-
WHOLE PLAICE 6.95
RED SNAPPER 7.50
LEMON SOLE 9.95
SALMON 7.95
GREY MULLET 7.25
TUNA STEAK 8.95
SWORDFISH STEAK 9.99
WHOLE TROUT 6.95
WHOLE SEA BASS 17.95

THE BAKER'S ARMS
SOMERFORD KEYNES, CIRENCESTER, GLOUCESTERSHIRE

Originally built in the 16th century, the pub has been extended and modernised during its life; part of the present building used to be the general shop for the village.

🔳 *11.30-2.30 (3.00 Sat), 6.30-11.00 Mon-Sat, 12.00-3.00, 7.00-10.30 Sun.*

🔳 *Courage Best, Mouldy Old Dough (house beer), Wadworth 6X, regular guest beer. Cider: Strongbow.*

🔳 *12.00-2.00 Mon-Sun, 7.00-9.00 Mon-Sat, 7.00 -8.30 Sun.* Ⓥ

SYMBOLS: 🅿 ❄ 👫 🔳

TEL: *01285 861298*

WHITE HART
18 HIGH ROAD, ASHTON KEYNES, WILTSHIRE

This fine old Cotswold pub was built in around 1750 and was originally known as the Cordwainer's Arms, a sign of shoemakers who used the Spanish leather cordwain. During the mid-19th century, the lords of the manors would hold the annual Court Leet in one of the upstairs rooms. At one time there was a skittle alley in the old stables, and before that the beer for the pub was brewed there.

🔳 *11.00-3.00, 5.00-11.00 Mon-Sat; 12.00-4.00, 7.00-10.30 Sun, April-Sept. Open all day during permitted hours.*

🔳 *Boddingtons Bitter, Fuller's London Pride, Wadworth 6X, White Hart Bitter (house beer), regular guest beer. Cider: Strongbow.*

🔳 *12.00-2.00 Mon-Sun, 5.30-9.30 Mon-Sat.* Ⓥ

SYMBOLS: 🅿 ❄ 👫 🔳 🔳 🔳 *(planned),* 🔳

TEL: *01285 861247*

Opposite Wild Duck Inn, Ewen

RED LION INN
HIGH STREET, CRICKLADE, WILTSHIRE

An old coaching inn, the Red Lion stands on the site of the old Norman Cricklade Mint, which was operational between the 10th and 12th centuries. The outbuildings were once part of bargees' cottages, which adds weight to the theory that the Thames used to be navigable beyond Lechlade up to Cricklade.

🕐 *11.00-2.30, 6.00-11.00 Mon-Sat; 12.00-2.30, 7.00-10.30 Sun. Open all day on Sat and Sun during summer.*
🍺 *Brains Bitter, Flowers IPA, Wadworth 6X. Cider: Strongbow.*
🍴 *12.00-2.00 Mon-Sun, 6.00-9.00 Mon-Sat, 7.00-9.00 Sun.* Ⓥ
SYMBOLS: 🌟 🍴 🕐 🏠 🍴
TEL: *01793 750776*

THE RED LION
THE STREET, CASTLE EATON, WILTSHIRE

Having the distinction of being the first pub actually on the banks of the Thames, this 18th-century hostelry retains all its original charm. Unusually for the area, it was built in red brick but with a Cotswold stone tile roof. Its large frontage may mean that the road in which it is sited used to be a lot busier than it is now. The interior has escaped the attention of the 'let's knock all the bars into one' brigade and still keeps the games room, lounge and snug bars.

The pub has a pètanque club, a variation on the French game of boules. Archaeological evidence suggests that a form of this game was played more than 7,000 years ago and it has even been said that this is what Sir Francis Drake was playing on the Hoe at Plymouth when the Spanish Armada was sighted. The play area, or piste as it is sometimes known, can be found in the side garden and a notice there advises of the piste fees per session.

Inside, you can play shove ha'penny, crib and table skittles. According to the landlord, crib is the only game where betting is allowed up to a round of drinks. Perhaps that's why all the customers play.

🕛 *12.00-3.00 Thurs-Sun (closed Mon, Tue, Wed lunchtimes during winter), 6.00-11.00 Mon-Sat, 7.00-10.30 Sun. Open all day during permitted hours in summer.*
🍺 *Ushers Best, Ushers Founders, Ushers Seasonal Ale. Cider: Blackthorn.*
🍴 *12.00-3.00 Mon-Sun, 6.00-10.00 Mon-Sat, 7.00-10.00 Sun.* Ⓥ
SYMBOLS: 🅿 ❄ 🚻 🐕 🏠 🍽
TEL: *01285 810280*

AXE & COMPASS
HIGH STREET, KEMPSFORD, GLOUCESTERSHIRE

This spartan pub was converted from three 15th-century cottages into an alehouse during the latter part of the 19th century. Then, it catered for the navvies who were working in the area, probably on either the Thames itself or the nearby Thames and Severn Canal.

🏛 *12.00-3.00, 7.00-11.00 Mon-Fri. Open all day during permitted hours on Sat and Sun.*
🍺 *Courage Best, Marston's Pedigree, occasional guest beer. Cider: Scrumpy Jack.*
🍽 *12.00-2.30, 7.00-9.30 Tues-Sun.* Ⓥ
Symbols: 🅿 ✳ 👫 🐾 🍴
TEL: *01285 810506*

THE GEORGE
HIGH STREET, KEMPSFORD, GLOUCESTERSHIRE

Typical of so many local village pubs, this two bar hostelry is the centre of a small community, its peace being broken only by the noise of planes at nearby RAF Fairford.

The George is first mentioned in Kempsford's history in 1758 and its title probably refers to the king of the time rather than the patron saint of England. In 1816 a certain Henry Phipps leased the premises from the Right Honourable George Hanger – Lord Coleraine – for an annual rent of 5 shillings. It

remained in the Phipps family for 27 years and then the inn had various tenants until Thomas Arkell, of the Swindon family brewer, took on the mortgage in 1861. It still remains part of their estate.

🏠 *11.00-3.00, 6.00-11.00 Mon-Sat; 12.00-3.00, 7.00-10.30 Sun. Open all day during permitted hours on Sat and Sun in summer.*
🍺 *Arkell's 2B & 3B. Cider: Strongbow.*
🍴 *12.00-2.00, 7.00-10.00 (9.00 Sun) every day except Tues.* ⓥ
SYMBOLS: 🅿 ❄ 🚹 🏠 🎐 🔁 *(planned),* 🏮
TEL: *01285 810236*

THE NEW INN HOTEL
MARKET SQUARE, LECHLADE, GLOUCESTERSHIRE

This three-storey Regency coaching inn lies within the shadow of the local church of St Lawrence. The poet Shelley visited Lechlade in 1815 and took a room at the New Inn. During his stay he wrote 'Stanzas in a Summer Churchyard'. The pathway from the churchyard to the river – now Shelley's Walk – was dedicated to him.

🏠 *11.00-3.00, 6.00-11.00 Mon-Sat; 12.00-3.00, 7.00-10.30 Sun.*
🍺 *Archers Best, Morland Original Bitter, regular guest beer. Cider: Strongbow.*
🍴 *Same as opening hours.* ⓥ
SYMBOLS: 🅿 ❄ 🚹 🏠 🎐 🔁
TEL: *01367 252296*

THE SWAN
BURFORD STREET, LECHLADE, GLOUCESTERSHIRE

Advertised as being the oldest pub in Lechlade, this fine Cotswold stone building was first mentioned in the Hockaday Absolutes, which contains copies of historical documents referring to Gloucestershire villages. It states that in 1513 'a tenement called

the Swan' was left in a will by Sir Robert Morton to his wife. In 1520 Sir Edward Tame, from a family of wool merchants and builders, constructed an inn on this site. Whether the original building was demolished or simply converted into a public house has not been detailed but the 1923 Trades Directory mentions the fireplace as dating back to 1520. At one time during its history, the pub was referred to as the White Swan but it has now reverted to its earlier name.

During its life it has fulfilled many functions, including that of a staging post for the Royal Mail and a resting place for the many passengers who came through Lechlade by horse-drawn coaches. This friendly pub still provides excellent food and refreshment, even a traditional English breakfast from an early hour – though you have to be content with a cup of tea to go with your meal until the clock strikes eleven.

11.00-11.00 Mon-Sat; 12.00-10.30 Sun.

Flowers Original, regular guest beer. Cider: Blackthorn.

Breakfast available 8.00-11.00 am (summer), 10.00-11.00 am (winter) Mon-Sun. Pub food menu available at all bar opening hours. ⓥ

SYMBOLS: 🅿 🛏 ⌨ ⚫ ⚫ ⚫ ⚫

TEL: *01367 253571*

THE TROUT INN
ST JOHN'S BRIDGE, LECHLADE, GLOUCESTERSHIRE

Y e Sygne of St John Baptist Head' was the name of this well-known inn until 1704, when it was changed to the Trout Inn. It started life as an almshouse to the Priory of Saint John the Baptist, which was dissolved by king Edward IV in 1472. Some of the remains of the priory are still visible in the garden. It controls two miles of ancient fishing rights that were originally granted by Royal Charter to the Brethren of the Priory.

The pub is sited at the junction of St John's Bridge where the River Leach joins the Thames. Across the bridge is St John's Lock, where the statue of Old Father Thames now rests, looking out over the boaters navigating this beautiful waterway.

This busy pub hosts many annual events, including the Tractor and Steam Engine Rally, traditionally held on the first weekend in June, the rule being 'bring anything old that goes.'

🍺 *10.00-3.00, 6.00-11.00 Mon-Sat; 12.00-3.00, 7.00-10.30 Sun. Open all day during permitted hours from spring to autumn.*

🛢 *Courage Best & Directors, occasional guest beer. Cider: Scrumpy Jack, Woodpecker.*

🍴 *12.00-2.30 Mon-Sun, 7.00-10.00 Mon-Sat, 7.00-9.30 Sun.* Ⓥ

SYMBOLS: 🅿 ✳ 👪 🐎 🏰 ✈ 🍴 🐾

TEL: *01367 252313*

Above The Trout Inn, Lechlade

THE PLOUGH INN
KELMSCOT, NR LECHLADE, GLOUCESTERSHIRE

This brightly coloured pub, built in 1631, is set in a slow-moving hamlet a short walk from the Thames. William Morris lived at Kelmscott Manor from 1871 until his death in 1896, though his contentment at his peaceful country retreat was threatened by scandal when Dante Gabriel Rossetti, a fellow artist and poet and one of his closest friends, was staying there. Rossetti fell in love with Morris's wife, Jane. She became the subject of much of his work and rumours of a mènage à trois escalated among the local population. Also, Rossetti's abusive behaviour, caused by his use of a primitive sleeping drug, increased his unpopularity and ultimately forced his departure.

The Plough served the community for many years until financial difficulties forced it to shut. It reopened in 1993 having been extensively modernised and improved, but retaining the old stone floors and oak beams. It is an excellent stopping-off point for walkers, cyclists and motorists, with free moorings available for those travelling by boat.

11.00-3.00, 6.00-11.00 Mon-Sat; 12.00-4.00, 7.00-10.30 Sun. Open all day during permitted hours from April to September.

Morland Original, regular guest beer. Cider: Scrumpy Jack, Woodpecker.

12.00-2.30 Mon-Sun, 7.00-9.30 Mon-Sun. Ⓥ

SYMBOLS: 🅿 ❄ 👥 🐕 🏠 🍴 🛏 ⚓

TEL: *01367 253543*

THE SWAN HOTEL
RADCOT BRIDGE, OXFORDSHIRE

This magnificent late 19th-century two-storey building is set by what is reputedly the oldest bridge on the Thames. Alongside the ancient bridge is a new crossing, built following a decision by the Thames Commissioners to provide a new cutting for the many barges using the river. To cater for the transportation of the Taynton stone from the local quarry, a wharf was also formed, which now is part of the pretty riverside gardens of the pub.

Internally the pub retains its association with the river and stuffed fish adorn the walls. To mark the pub's title they also have a stuffed swan, whose demise came about thanks to a fox in the mountain ranges of Wales. How it came to end up in a small village in Oxfordshire is not known.

The menu includes a vast range of dishes and the Swan is one of only a handful of pubs left that serves the seasonal delicacy of rook pie.

11.00-3.00, 6.00-11.00 Mon-Sat; 12.00-3.00, 7.00-10.30 Sun. Open all day during permitted hours in summer. Morland Original & Old Speckled Hen, regular guest beer. Cider: Strongbow. 12.00-2.00, 6.00-9.00 Mon-Fri; 12.00-3.00, 7.00-9.00 Sat & Sun.

SYMBOLS: P ❄ ♟ ☐ ⚑ ✏ ⛺ ☏

TEL: *01367 810220*

Above Handpumps in the Swan Hotel, Radcot Bridge

Above The Trout Inn, Buckland Marsh

THE TROUT INN
TADPOLE BRIDGE, BUCKLAND MARSH,
FARINGDON, OXFORDSHIRE

In the days before electricity had been installed, the lighting in this riverside inn (at one time kept by A Herring) was supplied by tilly lamps or candles. At that time the only way into the bottle cellar was through the ladies toilet and the landlord would go armed with a lamp, shouting as he went 'Is anybody in there?'

Another tale told is that the local police sergeant, who used to enjoy a tipple now and again, would call in at the pub while he was on duty. He would sit in the cellar hidden away from the public and his superiors. Invariably he would consume so much of his favourite beer that he could hardly stand by the end of the evening and the locals would have to sit him on his bike and push him home!

Now electricity has been installed, the local police have found better things to do and this friendly inn has built a reputation for good cask beer, wines and outstanding food.

🕐 *11.30-3.00, 6.00-11.00 Mon-Sat; 12.00-3.00, 7.00-10.30 Sun. Closed on Sunday evening from November to Easter.*

🍺 *Archers Best, Fuller's London Pride, regular guest beers. Cider: Bulmers, Scrumpy Jack.*

🍴 *12.00-2.00, 7.00 -9.00 Mon-Sun.* Ⓥ

SYMBOLS: 🅿 ❄ 👫 🎠 🏠 🍺 ☜

TEL: *01367 870382*

THE MAYBUSH
NEWBRIDGE, NR STANDLAKE, OXFORDSHIRE

The bridge at Newbridge was constructed by Benedictine monks in 1250, using stone from Taynton quarries, and it is rumoured that the cement was mixed with bull's blood. The bridge has stood the test of time, so there may some truth in this though the mortar does not look particularly red. After the monks had finished, they passed the care of the crossing into the hands of a hermit and its tollhouse was on the site of the inn. It is now free to cross the river and the anchorites were made redundant some years ago.

Nobody is quite certain how old this clean and tastefully decorated pub is, though it is widely believed to date back to the 16th century so it would certainly have been in existence in the Civil War when the Parliamentarians fought with soldiers from the Royal Garrison. Cromwell's troops won and the bridge was their prize.

At the rear, the garden looks out over the tranquil Thames and open fields where cows and sheep roam freely on the riverbanks, isolated from civilisation.

Once upon a time this side of the bridge was in Berkshire and crossing over would take you into the neighbouring county of Oxfordshire. In the days when the licensing laws were set by the counties and closing times were different, there used to be a rush across the bridge between the Maybush and the Rose Revived, where customers could have an extra 30 minutes' drinking time.

🍺 *11.30-3.00, 6.00-11.00 Mon-Sat; 12.00-3.00, 7.00-10.30 Sun. Open all day during permitted hours in summer.*

🍴 *Morland Original & Old Speckled Hen, occasional guest beer. Cider: Scrumpy Jack, Strongbow.*

🍽 *12.00-2.00, 6.30 (7.00 Sun)-9.00 Mon-Sun.* Ⓥ

SYMBOLS: 🅿 ❄ 🚻 🐾 ✕ 🕿

TEL: *01865 300624*

Above The Maybush, Newbridge

31

THE ROSE REVIVED
NEWBRIDGE, NR WITNEY, OXFORDSHIRE

There are many stories of how this large riverside inn with its weeping willows by the water received what must be the most romantic name in the country. One of the most delightful tales is that Oliver Cromwell, after a hard day directing his troops, needed some liquid refreshment and stopped at the inn. He noticed that the rose he was wearing was drooping, so he ordered an extra flagon of ale in which he placed his flower. After a short while both he and the rose were revived.

Another version is that in 1700 the inn was called Fayre House because of the twice-yearly carnival held in the adjacent field. Records from 1753 show that by now the name had changed to the Rose. A hundred years later it had again been altered, to the Rose & Crown. Lord Harcourt recorded in 1919 that when two knights of the realm, Sir Edmund Gross and Sir Hamo Thorneycroft, were both undergraduates at Oxford around 1870 they remembered the inn being called the Rose Revived and suggested it should revert to this name.

The pub is now run by a major chain and it can get extremely busy in the summer and at weekends; its position right by the Thames makes it one of the most popular venues around.

🔲 *11.00-11.00 Mon-Sat; 12.00-10.30 Sun.*
🍺 *Morland Original & Old Speckled Hen, Ruddles County.*
Cider: Strongbow.
🍽 *12.00-10.00 Mon-Sun.* Ⓥ
SYMBOLS: 🅿 ❄ 👫 🐾 🏠 🛏 ⬗ 🦜
TEL: *01865 300221*

THE RED LION
NORTHMOOR, OXFORDSHIRE

The short walk to this pub from the Thames will give the opportunity to see the lovely village of Northmoor. The inn was converted in 1754 from two 15th-century cottages and now epitomises the traditional local, with excellent ales, scrumptious food, real fires in the winter and even a piano player to tinkle the ivories on alternate Sunday lunchtimes. The dark torso of its resident apparition has been seen on three occasions by three different customers and the present landlord has himself experienced the odd bit of poltergeist-type mischief.

🔲 *12.00-3.00, 6.30-11.00 Mon-Sat; 12.00-3.30, 7.00-10.30 Sun.*
🔲 *Flowers Original, Morland Original, regular guest beer. Cider: Strongbow.*
🔲 *12.00-2.00 Mon-Sat, 12.00-3.00 Sun, 7.00-9.30 Mon-Sun.* Ⓥ
SYMBOLS: 🅿 ❄ 👪 🔲 🔲 🔲 🔲
TEL: *01865 300301*

THE PLOUGH
EATON ROAD, APPLETON, OXFORDSHIRE

In its heyday, this old coaching inn, built in 1683, was on the main Oxford to Swindon road. Thanks to the main A420, traffic through Appleton is now greatly reduced. The village pub was often used for other purposes and even doubled as the doctor's surgery for a number of years. Retaining its three bars, the pub has a wealth of character with its old wooden beams, low ceilings and age-stained walls.

🔲 *10.30-3.00, 6.00-11.00 Mon-Sat; 12.00-3.00, 7.00-10.30 Sun.*
🔲 *Morland Original, Ruddles Best. Cider: Strongbow.*
🔲 *12.00-2.00 Mon-Sun, 6.30-9.30 Mon-Sat, 7.00-9.00 Sun.* Ⓥ
SYMBOLS: 🅿 ❄ 👪 🔲 🔲 🔲 🔲
TEL: *01865 862441*

Opposite The Red Lion, Northmoor

Eaton
to
Burcot

From the small village of Eaton in the west of Oxfordshire, the river sets a course through green and peaceful countryside and soon reaches Bablock Hythe, an area mentioned in Matthew Arnold's poem 'The Scholar Gypsy'.

The foot passenger ferry has been in operation since AD 904. At one time it transported cars but nowadays, if you wish to cross the river in your car, you must take a short drive past the large reservoir at Farmoor to Swinford Bridge at Eynsham. This is one of the last two remaining toll bridges on the Thames. When it was built in 1769, by Lord Abingdon, the toll was set at one old penny per wheel, which is the equivalent of 2p per car, and remained at this rate until, in 1981, the new owner raised it to 5p, despite the opposition of the users of the bridge.

From here the river runs past Wytham Great Wood. Its six hundred acres of woodland belongs to Oxford University and is the habitat for a number of species of birds such as nightingales, teals and warblers. Passing by Duke's Cut, a waterway that links the Thames with the Oxford Canal, the river runs under the A34 trunk road. Soon the noise of traffic subsides and you are returned to the peace of the countryside.

Shortly afterwards the remains of Godstow Nunnery come into view. This is where Rosamund de Clifford, the mistress of Henry II, once lived. Queen Eleanor, jealous of her relationship with the king, poisoned Rosamund. She was buried at the nunnery in 1176 and her memory was preserved by the nuns, who elevated her to the position of a saint.

Next is Binsey, a small village with a handful of houses, a piece of grass that could loosely be described as a village green, a farm, a church and a pub. The first recorded vicar of the church was Nicholas Breakspear, who became Adrian IV when he was elected the first and only English Pope. Binsey is renowned for the Holy Well, which has healing powers according to the legend of the Virgin St Fredeswide. During the 8th century she was being chased through the Forest of Binsey by a man lusting after her. Due to a mysterious power he lost his sight, forcing him to give up the chase. But, on learning of his plight, St Fredeswide led him to the well and touched his eyes with the water. Miraculously, his sight was restored.

Within a short distance the river makes its entrance into Oxford, famed the world over for its monumental colleges, steeped in history and the achievements of its scholars past and present. You need plenty of time to explore this wonderful city, with its ancient buildings, abundance of pedal cycles, punts on the river, tourists and many traditions still observed by those who live or stay in Oxford.

On leaving the city, the Thames turns southwards and glides past Iffley, where can be found one of the finest examples of a Norman church, built around 1170. Some locks on the river lack beauty, this cannot be said about Iffley: a mill stream, wooden bridges, stone balustrade crossing and a charming lock-keeper's house all combine to present a perfect picture.

On to Sandford-on-Thames, renowned for its history of papermaking. It is here where the notorious weir pool has claimed a number of swimmers' lives. Marked by a stone memorial, all of the drowned have been undergraduates at Christ Church college: one of them being Michael Llewelyn Davies, one of the two brothers for whom Sir James Barrie wrote *Peter Pan*.

From Sandford the river becomes isolated from modern-day life until it reaches Abingdon. Saved from industrialisation by refusing to allow the Great Western Railway to pass through, Abingdon has survived as a market town for nearly a millennium and is saturated with history and old buildings. It was the county town of Berkshire until the boundaries were changed and now the town lies within Oxfordshire. The leisure centre was once the Old Gaol, built by French prisoners during the Napoleonic Wars.

The river follows the perimeter of the town before leaving on its way to Culham, best known for the 17th-century manor house with a mediaeval sundial and a large dovecote that can accommodate four thousand nesting birds.

Buried in the churchyard at Sutton Courtenay are Eric Arthur Blair, better known as the writer George Orwell, and Herbert Henry Asquith, the Liberal prime minister who, in 1908, while Chancellor of the Exchequer, introduced the old age pension. Also in the graveyard are the remains of Martha Pye, who died in 1832 at the age of 117.

The river leaves Culham Lock, and then the landscape opens up, revealing Didcot Power Station in all its modern glory. It flows on past Appleford and on to Long Wittenham, where the Clifton Cut bypasses the village. The atrtractive thatched cottages of Clifton Hampden soon come into view. It was a local character, William Dyke, who apparently fired the first shot at the Battle of Waterloo, though by all accounts he fired it by mistake.

Finally the small hamlet of Burcot is reached, though most of its houses are hidden from view.

Above The Trout Inn, Lower Wolvercote

THE EIGHT BELLS

EATON, NR ABINGDON, OXFORDSHIRE

This 15th-century pub started life as the Bells, named after the pendants that used to hang round the necks of working shire horses. It changed its name to the Six Bells after that many were installed in the local St Laurence's church. When it was decided to add another two to the belfry, the pub followed suit and became The Eight Bells, which name it retained even after the church added yet another set. The pub was supposedly visited at different times by both Charles I and Oliver Cromwell.

The natural cellar requires no cooling or heating due to it being below the water table; apparently there was a tunnel leading from it to the river at one time, though its purpose is not known.

Don't be put off by the pub's plain exterior as the interior is a masterpiece. There are two bars, each with its own distinct character. The lounge and restaurant has a wonderfully relaxed feel to it: the saloon, which resembles an old public bar, has high-backed seating, long bench tables and a long wooden bar.

Above The Eight Bells, Abingdon

🏛 *11.30-2.30, 6.00-11.00 Mon-Sat; 12.00-3.00, 7.00-10.30 Sun.*
🛢 *Morland Original, Ruddles Best, guest beer. Cider: Strongbow.*
🍽 *12.00-2.30 Tues-Sun, 7.00-9.30 Tues-Sat.* Ⓥ
SYMBOLS: 🅿 ❄ 👪 🎠 🏛 🥊 🍺
TEL: *01865 862983*

THE FERRYMAN INN
BABLOCK HYTHE, OXFORDSHIRE

Bablock Hythe has been an important ferry crossing for over a thousand years and there has been an inn on this site for hundreds of years. The pub started life as the Chequers before becoming the Ferry Inn (which name it still retains on the back of the building), then the Ferryman Inn.

The present building has undergone substantial modernisation works, so the success of the pub owes more to its position by the Thames than its appearance. The ferry is now operated by the pubs owners for foot passengers and cycles only.

🏛 *11.30-3.00, 7.00-11.00 Mon-Sat; 12.00-3.00, 7.00-10.30 Sun. Open all day during permitted hours on Sat and Sun in summer.*
🛢 *Greene King Abbot & IPA, occasional guest beer. Cider: Strongbow, Woodpecker.*
🍽 *12.00-2.00, 7.00-9.30 Mon-Sat; 12.00-2.30 Sun.* Ⓥ
SYMBOLS: 🅿 ❄ 👪 🎠 🥊 ➡ 🍺 ⊗
TEL: *01865 880028*

THE TALBOT
OXFORD ROAD, EYNSHAM, OXFORDSHIRE

The first recording of a tavern here was in 1769. Traders often met customers here to agree the price for their wares over a glass of beer or two.

From 1788 to 1821 it was called the Horse and Jockey, perhaps because of its close proximity to Port Meadow where horse racing took place for more than two hundred years. Its present name, which it was given in around 1836, indicates that hunting took place locally because talbots, the forerunners of the modern-day stag hound, were used for this purpose.

The front bar is named after Johnny Juggins, landlord from 1891 until he retired in 1940 at the age of 82.

Now that commercial traffic on the river has disappeared completely, this friendly, welcoming pub relies on custom from the many people who use the Thames for leisure pursuits, and passing trade from the motorists crossing the adjacent Swinford Toll Bridge.

🏠 *11.00-3.00, 5.30-11.00 Mon-Sat; 12.00-3.00, 7.00-10.30 Sun. Open all day during permitted hours from June to August.*
🍺 *Arkell's 2B, 3B & Kingsdown Ale. Cider: Strongbow.*
🍴 *12.00-2.00, 6.30 (7.00 Sun)-10.00 Mon-Sun.* ⓥ
SYMBOLS: 🅿 ❄ 🚻 🏠 ➡ 🍴
TEL: *01865 881348*

THE TROUT INN
195 GODSTOW ROAD, LOWER WOLVERCOTE, OXFORDSHIRE

This ivy-clad inn, with a large garden next to the weir, is one of the best-known and most famous pubs in the Oxfordshire area. It can be traced back to 1138 when it was built as a guest-house for the nearby Godstow Nunnery. Following the collapse of the monasteries in the early 16th century, it became a private house, finally being destroyed on the orders of Sir Thomas Fairfax, the Commander-in-Chief of the Parliamentary Army in the English Civil War. It is uncertain whether or not Godstow House, as it was then known, was totally obliterated but experts have dated the present building to the 17th century.

The pub has always been popular with Oxford University undergraduates and dons, one of whom was the mathematician the

Reverend Charles Lutwidge Dodgson, better known by his pen name of Lewis Carroll. It was in 1862 during a boating trip with the three young daughters of the Dean of Christ Church, one of whom was Alice Liddell, that he first narrated the story that would become *Alice in Wonderland*.

11.00-11.00 Mon-Sat; 12.00-10.30 Sun.
Draught Bass, Worthington Best Bitter. Cider: Blackthorn.
12.00-10.00 Mon-Sat; 12.00-9.00 Sun. Ⓥ
SYMBOLS: 🅿 ❋ 🚻 🐕 ⛲ 🍽 📶
TEL: *01865 554485*

Above The Trout Inn, Lower Wolvercote **Right** The Perch, Binsey

THE PERCH
BINSEY LANE, BINSEY, OXFORDSHIRE

There is some dispute over how long an inn has stood on this site, it could be anything from five to nine hundred years. One theory is that it was originally built as the living quarters for the stonemasons working on the reconstruction of St Margaret's church during the 12th century.

Perhaps because of its remote location, though only a short distance from the centre of Oxford, The Perch has suffered from several fires in its time. The present large building replaces the previous inn, which was destroyed by fire in 1977.

Many pubs can boast a resident ghost and this one is no exception. The spectre of a naval petty officer who lived locally can often be seen. He drowned himself in the river when he found himself deep in debt.

There is a giant chess board in the large pretty garden that looks on to the river.

🕒 *11.30-2.30 (3.00 Sat), 6.30 (6.00 Fri & Sat)-11.00 Mon-Sat; 12-3.00, 7.00-10.30 Sun. Open all day during permitted hours in summer.*

🍺 *Benskin's Best Bitter, Marston's Pedigree, Morland Old Speckled Hen (summer only), regular guest beer. Cider: Blackthorn.*

🍴 *12.00-2.00 Mon-Sun, 7.00-9.00 Mon-Sat; 12.00-9.00 summer weekends only.* Ⓥ

SYMBOLS: 🅿 ❄ 👫 �🏧 🍺 🍽 🐕

TEL: *01865 240386*

THE WATERMANS ARMS
7 SOUTH STREET, OSNEY ISLAND, OXFORD

Sandwiched between the Thames and a number of small tributaries, Osney Island, sometimes referred to by the locals as Frog Island because of its reputation for flooding, was first built on in the mid-

19th century following the building of the railway in 1852. At one time over a third of the local population worked on this new mode of transport. Travelling by road from Oxford through Osney at that time would have incurred a toll at the turnpike.

Built originally in the 1850s, this pub was named after the bargees who used to work the river. At the back of the building are the old stables where the barge horses would be kept overnight. In 1899 the pub was extended to cater for the additional river traffic caused by the opening of the Oxford Electric Light Station in 1892, which can still be seen on the bank opposite. The coal to power the generators would have been carried by boat.

The present landlady makes a range of delicious pies, using her own shortcrust pastry and local products where possible, all very good value for money.

📅 *11.00-3.00, 6.00-11.00 Mon-Fri. Open all day during permitted hours on Sat and Sun.*

🍺 *Morland IPA & Original. Cider: Scrumpy Jack, Strongbow.*

🍽 *12.00-2.00 Mon-Sun, 6.00-8.15 Mon-Sat.* Ⓥ

SYMBOLS: 🅿 ❄ 👪 🐕 🍴 ↻

TEL: *01865 248832*

THE HEAD OF THE RIVER
FOLLY BRIDGE, ST ALDATES, OXFORD

The Head of the River, next to Folly Bridge, has been a pub for more than 20 years. To help the developers choose a name, the Oxford Mail asked its readers for suggestions. The name was chosen from 2,700 entries and was based on the complicated Torpid's and Eight's Thames boat races in which the winner becomes Head of the River. The finishing line of this annual event is close by.

Until 1779 a tower stood on an island in the middle of the river. It had several uses and names. It was once the study and observatory of Friar Roger Bacon, a 13th-century philosopher and scientist whose knowledge far exceeded anyone else's of that period. It became known as the Folly when another storey was added. When the present bridge was built in 1827 it took its name from the former ornamental building. On the site there now stands a Venetian-style red brick building, dating from 1849, with female statues around the exterior and a strange-looking figure, said to resemble the devil, on the roof. It was once a house of ill-repute.

While the pub may be young, the stone building in which it is housed is not. Formerly known as the Wharf House, it was used as a warehouse for many years before becoming the boatyard for the long-established firm of Salter Brothers.

Now you can sit in the garden and watch punters on the river, both experienced and the inexperienced trying their hand for the first time. Inside the boating theme continues and there are numerous artefacts relating to life on the river.

🔳 *11.30-11.00 Mon-Sat; 12.00-10.30 Sun.*

🔳 *Fuller's Chiswick Bitter, ESB, London Pride. Cider: Scrumpy Jack.*

🔳 *12.00-9.00 Mon-Sun.* Ⓥ

SYMBOLS: ❄ 👬 🔳 🎦 🔁 🔊

TEL: *01865 721600*

THE ISIS TAVERN
IFFLEY LOCK, OXFORD

Isis, from the old Latin word for Thames – Tamesis – refers to the upper part of the river and some locals still call it by this name. This mid-Georgian building started life as a farmhouse around 1800 but was converted to an inn in 1842. It is one of the two pubs on the Thames that has no public vehicular access, so the only way to get there is on foot. The nicest route must be from the picturesque village of Iffley, across the lock, and then a short walk along the towpath towards Oxford.

Until recently it had been in the same family for nearly 80 years, having seen three generations of the Rose family. The beer used to be delivered by ferry, and a picture in the bar shows casks and bottles of beer being loaded on to the punt that was used to ferry the goods across the river. This method of transportation ended over 30 years ago and now all deliveries come down the towpath by electric handcart.

Old starting cannons are still used to begin the summer Torpid's and Eight's boat races, which start outside the Isis and finish at Folly Bridge, a course of over 1½ miles.

As you would expect, this large inn contains plenty of memorabilia and old black and white photographs reflecting life on the river. You can also try your hand on the old wooden nine-pin bowling alley

🔲 *11.00-11.00 Mon-Sat; 12.00-10.30 Sun.*
🔲 *Morrells Oxford Bitter & Varsity, Morrells Graduate, regular guest beer. Cider: Strongbow.*
🔲 *12.00-8.45 Mon-Sun.* Ⓥ
SYMBOLS: ❄️ 🕴️ 🐕 ♨️ 🎱 ⚓
TEL: *01865 247006*

THE FOX
25 HENLEY ROAD, SANDFORD-ON-THAMES, OXFORDSHIRE

This pub is one of the few places left that does not serve food and has no music, but it does have a reputation for selling the best and cheapest beer in the area. The now extinct Oxford brewer Morrells, which at one time owned the farm next door, built the pub over 160 years ago. The present tenants have run the place for three generations for over 80 years.

🕐 *12.00-3.00, 6.00-11.00 Mon-Sat; 12.00-3.00, 7.00-10.30 Sun.*
🍺 *Morrells Oxford Bitter & Varsity, regular guest beer.*
Cider: Strongbow.
SYMBOLS: 🅿 ❄ 🛏 ♨ 🍴
TEL: *01865 777803*

THE OLD ANCHOR INN
1 ST HELENS WHARF, ABINGDON, OXFORDSHIRE

Before 1884 the Anchor, as it was called then, was sited next to the wharf steps on the esplanade, It was seemingly no more than a hovel but it served the abundance of river workers who would have congregated in Abingdon. During the latter part of the 19th century the pub was rebuilt in its present position by the owners, Christs Hospital. Landlords at that time often had additional ways of earning a living and this was certainly the case here, as a photograph taken in 1892 proves. Mr Plownan not only served beer but also sold coal and hired out pleasure craft. So if you fancied a day on the river with a steam-driven boat and a flagon of ale, this was the place to go.

Entering this old Victorian inn, which has been extended over the years to its present size, reveals the modern setting of the front bar with

plush carpeting, cosy armchairs and pine tables. But by stepping a few places to the rear, a transformation takes place when you enter the snug with its combination of an old range, smoke-stained woodwork, flagstone floors and old bench seats.

11.00-11.00 Mon-Sat; 12.00-10.30 Sun.
Morland Old Speckled Hen & Tanners Jack. Cider: Strongbow.
12.00-2.00 Mon-Sun, 6.00-9.00 Mon-Sat. Ⓥ
SYMBOLS: ✳ 👫 🐕 🍲 📋 🚭
TEL: *01235 521726*

Above The Old Anchor Inn, Abingdon

THE BROAD FACE
BRIDGE STREET, ABINGDON, OXFORDSHIRE

Known as the Saracen's Head until around 1734, there are many apocryphal tales of how this pub became The Broad Face. Some say it symbolises the swollen face of a man drowning in the Thames, others the bloated face of a man hanged at the Old Gaol (unlikely as the gaol did not open until 1805).

🏠 *10.30-3.00, 6.00-11.00 Mon-Sat; 12.00-3.00, 7.00-10.30 Sun.*
🍺 *Morland Old Speckled Hen & Original, occasional guest beer.*
Cider: Strongbow.
🍴 *11.45-2.15, 6.00-9.30 Mon-Sat; 12.00-2.00 Sun.* ⓥ
SYMBOLS: 👬 🍴
TEL: *01235 524516*

THE PLOUGH
HIGH STREET, LONG WITTENHAM, NR ABINGDON, OXFORDSHIRE

In the early 1900s this village pub was known as the Paraffin Arms, this being the fuel used for all the cooking and heating before electricity. Over the years, the Plough has been used for many purposes, including a dairy, butcher's shop, slaughter house and venue for inquests.

The pub's garden is over 200 yards long, and leads right down to the river where free moorings are available.

🏠 *11.00-3.00, 5.00-11.00 Mon-Thurs; 11.00-11.00 Fri, Sat; 12.00-10.30 Sun. Open all day during permitted hours in summer.*
🍺 *John Smith's, Marston's Pedigree, Theakston Best Bitter. Cider: Strongbow.*
🍴 *12.00-2.30, 7.00-9.00 Mon-Sun.* ⓥ
SYMBOLS: 🅿 ❄ 👬 🐕 🍽 🗂 🍴 📷
TEL: *01865 407738*

THE VINE INN
HIGH STREET, LONG WITTENHAM, NR ABINGDON, OXFORDSHIRE

The thatched part of this building dates back to the 15th century and the brick-built extension was added in 1850, when it was recorded that the Vine was open for custom. Prior to this date, it served as a butcher's where the villagers would queue up in the adjacent lane waiting to be served their meat through a small hatch. In 1868, much of this old village was consumed by fire, but fortunately this pretty inn escaped the flames.

The outstanding interior decor which complements this small family-run pub is the work of a local artist, Nandi Ablett.

🕐 *11.00-11.00 Mon-Sat; 12.00-10.30 Sun.*
🍺 *Morland Old Speckled Hen & Original, Ruddles Best, occasional guest beer.*
Cider: Scrumpy Jack, Strongbow.
🍴 *12.00-2.00, 7.00-9.00 Mon-Sun.* Ⓥ
SYMBOLS: 🅿 ❄ 👬 🎫 ♿ 🍽
TEL: *01865 407832*

THE BARLEY MOW
CLIFTON HAMPDEN, NR ABINGDON, OXFORDSHIRE

This perfect inn can be reached by crossing the magnificent six-arched bridge at the picturesque village of Clifton Hampden. It is a fine example of a 14th-century building, with whitewashed walls, thatched roofs, low ceilings and small windows, constructed by the traditional 'cruck' method of a timber framework made of tree trunks. This type of construction is the oldest in England, most commonly seen in parts of the Midlands, but there are a number of fine examples in the Oxfordshire area.

The charming interior has retained the style of the period, with a labyrinth of rooms, exposed wooden beams, elaborate panelling and

antique tables with candles. An inglenook fireplace still remains where once the toll bridge keeper and his predecessor the ferryman would keep warm while waiting for any customers wishing to cross the river. The pub was once visited by Oliver Cromwell, while engaged with his troops in fighting the Royalists during the Civil War.

11.00-11.00 Mon-Sat; 12.00-10.30 Sun.

Courage Best & Directors, Theakston XB, regular guest beer - Wadworth 6X. Cider: Strongbow.

as opening hours. Ⓥ

SYMBOLS: 🅿 ❄ 🚻 🐕 🏠 🍺

TEL: *01865 407847*

THE PLOUGH INN
CLIFTON HAMPDEN, NR ABINGDON, OXFORDSHIRE

Sited on the main Abingdon to Dorchester road, part of the pretty thatched building dates back to the 14th century. It has retained many original features such as the exposed timber beams and inglenook fireplace. It is thought to have been originally built by a prosperous yeoman who first brewed beer for consumption by his friends, but soon began selling it to the public as well.

The John Hampden room is named after Oliver Cromwell's cousin, a politician whose ancestors once owned the village. During the

Opposite The Barley Mow, Abingdon

Civil War he naturally joined forces with the Parliamentarians, but was fatally wounded at Chalgrove Field, a mere five miles away.

If the exterior of this inn is enticing, then the interior will captivate you. The relaxed atmosphere and genial staff make any visit here a pleasure. The Plough is the only totally no-smoking inn featured in the book.

11.00-11.00 Mon-Sat; 12.00-10.30 Sun.
Courage Best & Directors, John Smith's. Cider: Strongbow.
as opening hours. Ⓥ
SYMBOLS: 🅿 ❄ 👫 🐴 🏠 🍴 ↪
TEL: *01865 407136/407811*

THE CHEQUERS
ABINGDON ROAD, BURCOT, OXFORDSHIRE

This 16th-century thatched inn escaped the fate of many of its counterparts until 1950 when the roof was completely destroyed by fire. Fortunately it was rebuilt to match the original. An extension was added in 1984 and now the large interior provides a pleasant setting with a grand piano that can be used by any budding musicians willing to show off their talents.

The comprehensive selection of food includes Granny Mott's steak and kidney pudding, made to the 1937 recipe of the landlady's grandmother, Dorothy Mottishead. The bread is baked freshly on the premises every day.

11.00-2.30, 6.00-11.00 Mon-Sat; 12.00-3.00, 7.00-10.30 Sun.
Brakspear Bitter, Wadworth 6X, two guest beers. Cider: Merrydown.
12.00-2.00 Mon-Sun, 6.30-9.00 Tues-Sat. Ⓥ
SYMBOLS: 🅿 ❄ 👫 🐴 🏠 🍴
TEL: *01865 407771*

Opposite The Chequers, Burcot

DORCHESTER-ON-THAMES

TO

LOWER SHIPLAKE

Despite its name, the abbey town of Dorchester is actually on the River Thame and not the Thames, which flows by a short distance away.

Before the bypass was installed, the high street formed part of the main road from Oxford to Henley and there would have been a steady flow of traffic through the town, with horse-drawn coaches stopping at the various coaching inns.

From here the Thames carries on through Shillingford, where the main street leads down to the river where there was once a wharf for the local village brewery.

Next is the Royal Borough of Wallingford, which at one time had 62 pubs, though there are far fewer now. The churches have also suffered: in the 12th century there were thought to be 14 but now there are only three. The crime writer Agatha Christie lived nearby for many years. Crowmarsh Gifford, across Wallingford Bridge, was thought to have been owned by Walter Gifard, probably awarded to him in recognition of his services as standard bearer to William the Conqueror in the 11th century.

Now flowing in a southerly direction, the Thames runs through the villages of North Stoke, Cholsey, Moulsford and South Stoke until it reaches the attractive town of Goring. Goring's church of St Thomas of Canterbury has one of the oldest bells in the country, reputedly cast around 1290. Before the bridge was built, passage to the opposite bank was by ferry. In 1674, after an annual feast and a day full of good cheer with plenty of ale and wine, 60 people including children and a mare boarded the ferry, which clearly was not meant for so many. During the crossing the ferry tragically plunged over the weir leaving few survivors.

A bridge was later installed at Goring and crossing here will take you over the county line into the Royal Berkshire village of Streatley. There are wonderful panoramic views across the Thames Valley from the top of Streatley Hill.

From this point the Thames enters the Chilterns, designated by the National Trust as an area of 'outstanding natural beauty'. The writer Robert Gibbings once said that this middle section of the river was crowded with views that 'might have dropped from gold frames at the Royal Academy'.

The churchyard at Lower Basildon contains the body of Jethro Tull, inventor of the seed drill which eventually revolutionised the agricultural industry. Coming next are the grounds and house of Basildon Park and the bird sanctuary of Beale Park, before the river enters Pangbourne. Kenneth Grahame, best known as the author of *The Wind in the Willows*, lived here from 1924 until his death in 1932.

Across the water lies Whitchurch-on-Thames, reached by crossing the second toll bridge on the Thames. Flowing on, the countryside bordering one side of the river starts to be replaced with houses, factories and warehouses before the entry into Caversham, a fairly modern town that developed mainly in the 19th century. The river bypasses the large town of Reading and, thankfully, soon enters green countryside once again.

Soon the delightful village of Sonning appears, whose past can be traced back to Anglo-Saxon times. It was at one stage owned by the Bishops of Salisbury, who would stay in the palace at Holme Park, which survived until the reign of Queen Elizabeth I.

From here the Thames changes direction and sets a northerly course through the Berkshire town of Wargrave. Thomas Day, a writer who believed in taming animals by kindness, was buried in the churchyard having been killed when his horse threw him! Madame Marie Tussaud, the French wax modeller, is also laid to rest here.

On the opposite side of the river lies Shiplake. Alfred, Lord Tennyson married Emily Smallwood in the church of St Peter and St Paul in 1850, in the same year that he was created poet laureate.

FLEUR DE LYS INN
HIGH STREET, DORCHESTER-ON-THAMES, OXFORDSHIRE

A 16th-century timber-framed coaching inn thought to have been built by French prisoners of war, which may help explain the origin of its name. Once the village blacksmith's and bakery, it would have been one of many inns in Dorchester that served customers travelling by coach from London to Oxford in the 18th century.

Sitting opposite the Abbey Church and Rotten Row, this small free house sits in a long-standing terrace of residential houses that line the High Street. The small entrance set into the black and white exterior leads into a bar where little has changed over the years and local characters mingle with visitors in perfect harmony.

🕐 *11.00-2.30 (3.00 Wed-Sat), 6.30-11.00 Mon-Sat; 12.00-3.00, 7.00-10.30 Sun.*
🍺 *Draught Bass, Flowers IPA, Mansfield Bitter. Cider: Strongbow.*
🍴 *12.00-2.00 Mon-Sun, 7.00-9.30 Mon-Sun (not Sun evening in winter).* Ⓥ
SYMBOLS: 🅿 ❄ 🚻 🎏 🍴
TEL: *01865 340502*

THE KINGFISHER
27 HENLEY ROAD, SHILLINGFORD, OXFORDSHIRE

D on't be put off by the tarnished exterior of this truly free house on the Henley to Oxford road, a popular and picturesque route through Oxfordshire. Its change of name from the New Inn probably came about because kingfishers can frequently be seen on this stretch of river.

🕐 *11.00-11.00 Mon-Sat; 12.00-4.00, 7.00-10.30 Sun.*
🍺 *regular guest beer. Cider: Blackthorn.*
🍴 *12.00-3.00, 6.30 (7.00 Sun)-10.00 Mon-Sun.* Ⓥ
SYMBOLS: 🅿 ❄ 🚻 🎏 🍴 🚭 ✂
TEL: *01865 858595/858286*

THE COACHMAKER'S ARMS
37 ST MARYS STREET, WALLINGFORD, OXFORDSHIRE

This 17th-century Grade II listed building on the edge of town did not make an appearance in the licensing register until 1872, so it is unclear whether or not it sold beer before that date. In 1846 the premises were occupied by George Williams, a saddler and harness maker. It was common then for a landlord to have more than one trade, with the brewing often being done by the woman of the house. It had various owners until it became part of the Goring-based

Gundry's Brewery Estate. Sadly, this company ceased trading in 1941 and the pub was purchased by its present owner, the Henley brewer W.H.Brakspear & Sons. A conventional drinking house that provides a welcoming atmosphere.

🕅 *12.00-2.30, 5.30-11.00 Mon-Sat; 12.00-3.00/4.00, 7.00-10.30 Sun.*
🍺 *Brakspear Bitter & Special. Cider: Strongbow.*
🍴 *12.00-2.30 Mon-Sun (sandwiches and light snacks only).*
SYMBOLS: ❋ ♟ 🦌 ➋ ♨
TEL: *01491 839382*

QUEEN'S HEAD
72 THE STREET, CROWMARSH GIFFORD, WALLINGFORD, OXFORDSHIRE

One of the oldest pubs in Oxfordshire, being built sometime around the 13th century, it started its life as the Three Cocks. Oliver Cromwell is said to have taken refuge here and concealed himself in the chimney recess on the night before the assault

on Wallingford Castle. It was renamed as the Queen's Head in 1767, possibly after Charlotte of Mecklenburg, wife of George III.

Inside is a large aisled hall with wooden balconies, thought to be part of the original construction. The remainder of the spacious interior also presents an olde worlde feel with its exposed beams and brickwork, large fireplace and good old-fashioned service.

🔲 *12.00-11.00 Mon-Sat; 12.00-10.30 Sun. Closed 3.00-5.00 Mon-Thurs in winter.*

🔲 *Brakspear Bitter, Hampshire Arthur Pendragon, occasional guest beer. Cider: Blackthorn.*

SYMBOLS: 🅿 ❋ 🚻 🏠 🍺 🍽

TEL: *01491 834827*

The Perch & Pike
SOUTH STOKE, OXFORDSHIRE

South Stoke's only remaining pub was extremely popular with the locals in the early part of the 20th century. It would open at seven in the morning and stay open until ten in the evening, with beer at only 2d a pint. A double blow was served with the advent of the First World War: beer was increased to 3d and a restriction on opening hours was introduced.

Part of the brick and flint building dates back to the 17th century, these materials having been popular in the area at that time. In 1887 it was known as the Bricklayers Arms, having changed from the Perch & Pike, but by 1940 it had reverted to its original name. The Henley brewer, Brakspear's, acquired the premises in 1941 following the closure of the brewery at Goring.

Above The Perch and Pike, South Stoke

The inn was extensively and tastefully renovated in 1992. The light and spacious feel in the main bar is complemented by the antique furniture, including an old grandfather clock, and tasteful decorations. The short but mouthwatering menu is changed every two months.

🕮 *12.00-2.30, 6.00-11.00 Mon-Sat; 12.00-3.00 Sun. Closed Sun evening.*
🍺 *Brakspear Bitter & Special, occasional guest beer. Cider: Strongbow.*
🍴 *12.00-2.00 Mon-Sun; 7.00-9.15 Mon-Sat.* Ⓥ
SYMBOLS: 🅿 ✳ 🕴 🏠 ♨ ✕
TEL: *01491 872415*

THE CATHERINE WHEEL
STATION ROAD, GORING-ON-THAMES, OXFORDSHIRE

Dating back to the 16th century, this lovely Elizabethan inn is said to be the oldest building in Goring. When the road outside was the main thoroughfare through the village, the horse-drawn coaches would stop here, not only for the passengers to seek refreshment, but to use the forge next door. Both the inn and the forge were owned by the Critchfield family and, when the smithy finally closed, its buildings were incorporated into the inn.

The pub was once owned by Ann Gundry, the eccentric owner of the brewery in Goring who used to walk around the town with a shopping bag full of one pound notes. As happened to many of the other Gundry pubs in the locality, The Catherine Wheel was purchased by Brakspear's following the closure of the brewery. Now it is one of the few outlets where the whole range of their beers can be found and has a reputation for the way they are kept and served.

Above right The Catherine Wheel, Goring-on-Thames

Look out for the house leeks on the sloping roof by the main entrance. They are there because they are thought to keep witches at bay!

🎞 *11.30-2.30 Mon-Fri, 12.00-3.00 Sat, 6.00-11.00 Mon-Sat; 12.00-3.00, 7.00-10.30 Sun.*
🍺 *Brakspear Bitter, Mild, Old Ale & Special, Brakspear seasonal beer. Cider: Stowford Press.*
🍽 *12.00-2.00 Mon-Sun, 7.00-9.30 Mon-Sat.* ⓥ
SYMBOLS: ❄ 👫 🔥 🍴 ➡ 🍽
TEL: *01491 872379*

THE BULL AT STREATLEY
READING ROAD, STREATLEY, BERKSHIRE

This old inn on the Reading to Oxford Road has been a focal point in Streatley village for over five hundred years. Surprisingly, it did not form part of the Morrell Brewery estate, which owned many of the surrounding buildings.

The interior was refurbished in 1997, but still retains the charm you would expect from a historic inn. There has been little change to the exterior over the years, with even the old water pump at the front of the inn still working hundreds of years after it was first built. The two yew trees in the garden, it is said, mark the spot where two forbidden lovers perished in the 1500s. A young monk and his love, a nun from a nearby convent, used the inn for their assignations. They were eventually discovered, killed and buried in the unconsecrated ground of the pub's garden.

 *11.30-2.30 Mon-Thurs, 11.30-3.00 Fri & Sat, 6.00-11.00 Mon-Sat;
12.00-3.00, 7.00-10.30 Sun.*

 *Courage Best, Pope's Traditional, Royal Oak, regular guest beer.
Cider: Blackthorn.*

 *12.00-2.00 Mon-Sun, 7.00-9.15 Mon-Sat.* ⓥ

SYMBOLS: 🅿 ❄ 👫 🐕 🏠 ➡

TEL: *01491 872392*

THE CROWN
READING ROAD, LOWER BASILDON, BERKSHIRE

There has been a public house on this site since the beginning of the 19th century. For many years it was a thatched house known as the Old Mary Ann after the landlady, Mrs Mary Ann Robinson. She ran the pub single-handedly from the 1830s until the 1870s and during this time had it rebuilt to form the structure that stands today.

With its commanding views over the Goring Gap, this large pub is a good place to stop for lunch or dinner and to enjoy the scenery of the Thames Valley.

⏲ *11.00-3.00, 6.00-11.00 Mon-Sat; 12.00-10.30 Sun.*
🍺 *Morland Original & Old Speckled Hen, Ruddles Best. Cider: Strongbow.*
🍽 *11.30-2.30, 6.00-9.30 Mon-Sat; 12.00-4.00 Sun (variable in summer).* Ⓥ
SYMBOLS: 🅿 ❄ 🚻 🔗 🔄 🍴
TEL: *01491 671262*

THE SWAN
SHOOTER HILL, PANGBOURNE, BERKSHIRE

Overlooking the weir at Pangbourne, this 17th-century inn has recently been modernised to cater for the many customers who flock to this busy riverside location. Kenneth Grahame, who lived in the town for the latter part of his life, is reputed to have written the majority of *The Wind in the Willows* in the bar.

The boundary line between the counties of Oxfordshire and Berkshire used to go right through the middle of this old building, dividing the two bars. The licensing laws were different in the two regions and closing time would vary by half an hour. Any customers who wanted to extend their drinking time simply moved from one county to the other by taking their drink into the other bar!

🔲 *11.00-11.00 Mon-Sat; 12.00-10.30 Sun.*
🍺 *Morland Old Speckled Hen, Ruddles Best. Cider: Strongbow.*
🍴 *12.00-10.00 Mon-Sun.* Ⓥ
SYMBOLS: 🅿️ ❄️ 👫 🔲 🍽️ 🐾 ⛵
TEL: *0118 984 4494*

THE GREYHOUND
HIGH STREET, WHITCHURCH-ON-THAMES, OXFORDSHIRE

Establishing the age of old buildings is often difficult, and the Greyhound is no exception. It is certain, though, that the building started life as three cottages, one of which housed the local ferryman, Nathan Bushnell. His wife would brew beer in the back of the cottage for Nathan to sell to his many customers crossing the water from Pangbourne.

The building became a pub in 1830 and was first owned by the local brewer, Blatch's of Theale, with the beer being delivered by horse and cart. The police dealt with anyone who became drunk by locking them up in the shed at the side of the pub. There they would stay overnight to sober up before being chained to one of the famous 19 pollarded elm trees of Whitchurch, and some were even flogged for their misdemeanours.

The pub lies in a building conservation area, and the practice of keeping things as they were extends inside the pub. There is a policy of no music, fruit machines or even the serving of chips, which is popular with many of today's customers.

🔲 *11.30-2.30, 6.00-11.00 Mon-Sat; 12.00-2.30, 7.00-10.30 Sun.*
🍺 *Flowers IPA & Original, Marston's Pedigree, Wadworth 6X, regular guest beer. Cider: Blackthorn.*
🍴 *12.00-1.30 Mon-Sun, 7.00-9.00 Mon-Sat.* Ⓥ
SYMBOLS: 🅿️ ❄️ 🔲
TEL: *0118 984 2160*

CROSS KEYS
CHURCH ROAD, PANGBOURNE, BERKSHIRE

Now over four hundred years old, this Grade II listed building was at one time two private residences and the hallway inside, with an old stone floor, the alleyway between them.

The sign of the Cross Keys is one of the oldest British pub names. Because of the religious connotations, the majority of these were changed at the time of the Reformation. It is thought that this hostelry acquired its name because the keys of the local parish church of St James the Less were lodged at the inn and anyone wishing to enter would collect the keys from here.

🛏 *11.00-11.00 Mon-Sat; 12.00-10.30 Sun.*
🍺 *Charles Wells Bombardier, Morland Independent & Old Speckled Hen, Ruddles Best. Cider: Blackthorn.*
🍽 *12.00-2.30 Mon-Sun, 6.30-9.00 Mon-Sat.* ⓥ
SYMBOLS: ❄ 👫 🐎 🎮 ➡ 🍽
TEL: *0118 984 3268*

Above The Greyhound, Whitchurch-on-Thames

THE GRIFFIN

10/12 CHURCH ROAD, CAVERSHAM, READING, BERKSHIRE

An inn has stood on this site since the early 17th century, but unfortunately the old structure was demolished in 1911 to make way for the building that stands today. Old black and white photographs exhibited inside show the inn as it used to be.

A griffin is a mythical monster formed from two mighty creatures, the eagle and the lion, with the strength and greatness of each animal. The sign of the griffin was part of the coat of arms of Lord Craven, Lord of the Manor at Caversham from 1633 to 1688 and said to be the first owner of the inn.

The inn boasts a large garden in the shadow of Caversham bridge that leads right down to the banks of the Thames. At one time, eels were common on this stretch of the river in season and eel stew a regular feature on the menu.

🕐 *11.00-11.00 Mon-Sat; 12.00-10.30 Sun.*
🍺 *Courage Best & Directors, Theakston Best, regular guest beer.*
Cider: Strongbow.
🍽 *11.00-10.00 Mon-Sat; 12.00-9.30 Sun.* Ⓥ
SYMBOLS: 🅿 ❋ 🚻 🏠 🕎 🏕
TEL: *0118 947 5018*

PIPER'S ISLAND BAR
BRIDGE STREET, CAVERSHAM, READING, BERKSHIRE

It is said that an old fisherman named Piper used to reside on an island next to Caversham Bridge. When the bridge was due to be rebuilt they needed to move old Mr Piper, but stubbornly he refused to budge. Faced with the dilemma, the builders brought in two river barges moving his house twenty yards, while he was still in it. The old fisherman, if he ever existed, has long since gone and his house demolished to make way for the present structure of the pub.

🕐 *12.00-3.00 Mon-Sun, 5.00-11 Mon-Sat, 7.30-10.30 Sun. Open all day during permitted hours on Sat and Sun in summer.*
🍺 *Brakspear Bitter, guest beer changed every three months. Cider: Strongbow.*
🍽 *12.00-2.30, 6.00-9.30 Mon-Fri; 12.00-5.00, 6.00-9.30 Sat, Sun.* Ⓥ
SYMBOLS: ❋ 🚻 🏠 🏕 🍽 ♨
TEL: *0118 948 4573/4*

THE BULL INN
HIGH STREET, SONNING-ON-THAMES, BERKSHIRE

The history of this late 14th-century country inn is very much linked to that of the local church of St Andrew's and it in fact still forms part of the church estate. Originally called the Church House, it started life as a hostelry for the pilgrims who had travelled to Sonning to be blessed by 'St Sarlic' – a corruption of Sigeric, the Saxon Bishop of Sonning. In later years it became the venue for celebrations when the Bishop of Salisbury visited. A lavish feast would be provided with copious amounts of wine, and the celebratory festivities often lasted for several days.

During the reign of Elizabeth I, an exchange of properties was made with the Bishop of Salisbury, with Sonning passing to the Crown estate in exchange for Warlingham. The Crown appointed Sir Henri Nevill as Lord Steward to oversee the village and its affairs. His coat of arms featured a black bull and, in his honour, the inn was renamed.

The pub was tastefully restored and refurbished in 1995 by the brewers George Gale. It retains all the atmosphere and features you would expect from an inn of this age. It offers excellent food, superb Gales beers and old English country wines.

🕰 *11.00-3.00, 5.30 (6.00 Sat)-11.00 Mon-Sat; 12.00-3.00, 7.00-10.30 Sun.*
Open all day during permitted hours on Sat and Sun in summer.
🛢 *Brakspear Special, Gale's Butser, GB & HSB, regular guest beer.*
Cider: Strongbow.
🍴 *12.00-2.00, 6.30-9.00 Mon-Fri; 12.00-9.00 Sat, Sun.* Ⓥ
SYMBOLS: 🅿 ❄ 👪 🐕 ✈ 🍴 ⬇, 🍴
TEL: *0118 969 3901*

Above The Bull Inn, Sonning-on-Thames

THE BULL HOTEL
HIGH STREET, WARGRAVE, READING, BERKSHIRE

This brick-built hotel was constructed in the 15th century as a coaching in. Today it is renowned for its good food and well-kept Brakspear's beers.

🔲 *11.00-3.00, 6.00-11.00 Mon-Sat; 12.00-4.00, 7.00-10.30 Sun.*
🔲 *Brakspear Bitter & Special. Cider: Strongbow.*
🔲 *12.00-2.00, 7.00-9.30 Mon-Sat; 12.00-3.00 Sun.* Ⓥ
SYMBOLS: 🔲 🔲 🔲 🔲 🔲 🔲
TEL: *0118 940 3120*

THE GREYHOUND
HIGH STREET, WARGRAVE, READING, BERKSHIRE

Parts of this ivy-clad brick building date from the early 18th century. Over the years, this outstanding pub has been altered and extended, but it still retains two bars and a snug with a large open fireplace. At one time the Greyhound was used as the Magistrates Court. Situated at the rear is an old forge once used by the blacksmith to shoe horses bought in by the local farmers and travellers, who would park their horse-drawn vehicles in the yard at the back of the pub. The present landlord has turned the forge into a working museum, open mainly during the summer, providing a wonderful opportunity to see a smithy in operation. The lounge bar houses a collection of more than three hundred water jugs of every shape and size.

🔲 *11.00-11.00 Mon-Sat; 12.00-10.30 Sun.*
🔲 *Courage Best, regular guest beer. Cider: Taunton.*
🔲 *12.00-2.00, Mon-Sun.* Ⓥ
SYMBOLS: 🔲 🔲 🔲 🔲 🔲
TEL: *0118 940 2556*

Opposite The Greyhound, Wargrave

THE BASKERVILLE ARMS
STATION ROAD, LOWER SHIPLAKE, NR HENLEY-ON-THAMES,
OXFORDSHIRE

Thought to be one of only two pubs in England with this name. The sign outside shows the Baskerville coat of arms, a family who at one time owned most of the surrounding land and lived at the grand Crowsley Park.

This large brick-built pub, constructed in 1937, started life as a small country hotel in the comparatively young village of Lower Shiplake. It was tastefully renovated in 1998 and now serves a mixture of locals and visitors to the area.

🕑 *12.00-3.00, 6.00-11.00 Mon-Sat; 12.00-3.00, 7.00-10.30 Sun.*
🍺 *Brakspear Bitter, regular guest beers. Cider: Strongbow.*
🍽 *12.00-2.00, 6.00 (7.00 Sun)-9.00 Mon-Sun.* Ⓥ
SYMBOLS: 🅿 ❄ 🧑 🐴 🛏 ➡ 🎣
TEL: *0118 940 3332*

HENLEY-ON-THAMES
TO
WINDSOR

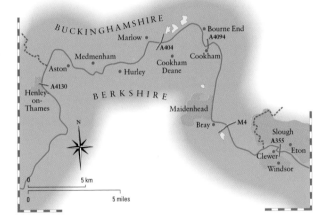

Henley-on-Thames was described by Charles Dickens as the 'Mecca of the rowing man'. It is most famous for its annual Royal Regatta but in 1829 it was also the venue for the first Oxford and Cambridge boat race before it moved to London.

The town boasts the river and some fine pubs and is also home to Brakspear's Brewery, established in 1779. If you happen to be in town on a brewing day, you will sample the aromas of beer-making wafting overhead.

From Henley Bridge, the course of the river is straight until it reaches Temple Island, now best known as the starting point for the Regatta course. The island's famous Folly, with a base like a small cottage and columned tower rising up from the roof has overlooked the river like a lighthouse since it was built in 1771 by the architect James Wyatt.

The Thames flows on through Hambleden, its 16th-century water mill now clad in white weatherboarding to disguise the flats inside. This area is considered to be one of the prettiest parts of the river.

From here the river turns eastwards and soon reaches Medmenham, once a ferry crossing. Medmenham Abbey was home to the renowned Hellfire Club, founded in 1745 by Sir Francis Dashwood. With its motto being 'do what thou wilt', the abbey has undoubtedly seen its share of strange events.

Further up river is the village of Hurley, where can be seen the remains of an 11th-century priory, founded by Geoffrey de Mandeville after the Norman Conquest.

Past Bisham, the Thames reaches Marlow. The best views of the river, weir and lock are from the ornate white suspension bridge, built in 1831 by Tierny Clark, and a gentle stroll up the tree-lined high street will reveal a town steeped in history. Marlow's oldest building is thought to be the Old Parsonage of 14th-century origin with panelled internal walls. Percy Bysshe Shelley wrote his epic poem 'The Revolt of Islam' in Albion House nearby, while his second wife, Mary Godwin, was creating Frankenstein. T.S. Eliot, the American poet, lived in West Street for a short time after the Second World War.

The Thames leaves Marlow as silently as it entered and passes Cookham Deane on the right, hidden from view by the mighty beech woods. Soon Bourne End comes into view. Across the water lies busy Cookham with its high street full of shops and restaurants. The artist

Above The Angel on the Bridge, Henley-on-Thames

Stanley Spencer found fame by recreating the story of Christ in this village, where he was born and lived. With his thin, bony frame and wild hair, he would often be seen pushing a pram containing his painting materials. He would stop when he liked, set up his easel and place a notice that read, 'Mr Spencer would be grateful if visitors would kindly avoid distracting his attention from his work.'

From Cookham, the river passes the grand house of Cliveden, once home to the Astor family, notorious for its part in the Profumo Scandal of 1963. It is now a hotel, with the grounds under the care of the National Trust.

From here to Bray, there is a dearth of riverside pubs. The houses on the banks are occupied by the rich and famous. The village of Bray, with its impeccable layout and fine Georgian houses, would have seen its fair share of Hollywood greats too – Walt Disney, David Niven and Errol Flynn – as they visited the nearby Bray Film Studios.

Flowing on, the river now starts its gradual descent to Eton and Windsor, passing Dorney, Boveney, Windsor Racecourse (which is effectively on an island) and Clewer.

On entering Windsor, one soon sees the mighty castle overlooking the town, one of the many homes of the sovereigns of Great Britain. It was built on a high chalk ridge by William the Conqueror over nine hundred years ago, though he never actually lived there, preferring his palace at Old Windsor. The Round Tower was added by Henry II, and further additions and enlargements took place over the years including the remodelling by the architect Jeffrey Wyatville, commissioned by George IV in the 1830s. In 1992, a fire broke out in the private chapel, quickly spreading to cause serious damage. The castle has been painstakingly restored by master craftsmen and is once again open to the public.

Crossing Windsor Bridge you'll find Eton, famous for its public school and exquisite college buildings. The college was founded by Henry VI in 1440 and, at the last count, 20 future British prime ministers had been through the school as well as countless royals. Eton has a good selection of pubs, restaurants and shops selling old books and antiques.

THE ANCHOR INN
58 FRIDAY STREET, HENLEY-ON-THAMES, OXFORDSHIRE

Before it became a thoroughfare, Friday Street was the site of a stream that flowed down to the Thames, providing fish to the townsfolk for the traditionally meatless day of the week. At one stage in the 16th century, it was Henley's red-light district, far removed from its social standing today.

The Anchor used to be the brewery tap for the Grey's brewery estate, a company formed in 1823 operating from premises in Friday Street. Because of financial problems, Grey's was purchased by its local rival, W.H. Brakspear & Sons, in 1896, the sale including the pub estate.

In a town that boasts a number of drinking establishments, this is certainly one not to be missed. The staff are friendly, as is Cognac, the ice-cube-eating dog. It's popular with the rowing fraternity and has plenty of associated memorabilia adorning the walls. The enclosed rear garden has a grapevine and an abundance of colourful flowers in the summer.

11.00-11.00 Mon-Sat; 12.00-10.30 Sun.

Brakspear Bitter & Special, occasional Brakspear seasonal beer. Cider: Scrumpy Jack.

12.00-3.00 Mon-Sun; 6.00-9.00 Mon-Sat. Ⓥ

SYMBOLS: 🅿 ❋ 👫 🍽

TEL: *01491 574753*

Above The Anchor Inn, Henley-on-Thames

THE ANGEL ON THE BRIDGE
THAMESIDE, HENLEY-ON-THAMES, OXFORDSHIRE

Possibly the best-known pub in Henley due to its prime location by the bridge. Built in the 17th century, this three-storey structure rises above the Thames crossing, presenting its fine old exterior to all those who arrive by road from the Berkshire side.

It is very popular in the good weather months with those people who like to watch the river traffic and soak up the atmosphere, but beware if the river is in flood as you may get your feet wet.

The modern-looking interior is perhaps not what you would expect from a building that appears so old from the outside, though the contemporary menu will delight even the harshest of critics.

🕰 *11.00-11.00 Mon-Sat; 12.00-10.30 Sun.*
🍺 *Brakspear Bitter, occasional Brakspear seasonal beer. Cider: Strongbow.*
🍴 *12.00-2.30 Mon-Fri; 12.00-3.30 Sat, Sun; 6.00-10.00 Mon-Sat.* ⓥ
SYMBOLS: ❄ 🚻 🏠 🍴 🔌 🚭
TEL: *01491 410678*

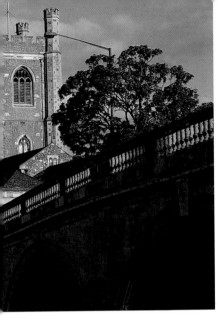

THE ROSE & CROWN
56 NEW STREET, HENLEY ON THAMES, OXFORDSHIRE

The history of this old coaching inn can be traced back to the mid-17th century, when Henley was an important stopping point on the main Oxford to London highway. An association with the Quakers was established in 1658, when Ambrose Rigg started preaching the doctrine at the Corn Market, having stabled his horse at the inn. Local legend has it that a series of underground tunnels linking various buildings once existed in the town; there is a blocked-up passage in the cellar at the Rose & Crown, believed to have been an escape route to nearby Phyllis Court for those trying to escape the long arm of the law.

It is one of the closest pubs to Brakspear's Brewery, but was owned until 1941 by the Goring Brewery. Brakspear purchased their competitor's pub estate, including the Rose & Crown, when they went out of business.

Two windows on the front exterior appear to have been blocked up when window tax was first levied in 1789 and were not reopened when the tax was repealed in 1851. Inside is a small but hospitable bar with a good menu and a piano anyone is welcome to use. The remains of an old well can be seen in the middle of the floor.

11.00-3.00, 6.00-11.00 Mon-Sat; 12.00-3.00, 7.00-10.30 Sun.

Brakspear Bitter & Special, Brakspear seasonal beer. Cider: Scrumpy Jack.

12.00-2.30 Mon-Sun, 7.00-9.30 Mon-Sat. Ⓥ

SYMBOLS: ❄ 🏠 ↗

TEL: *01491 578376*

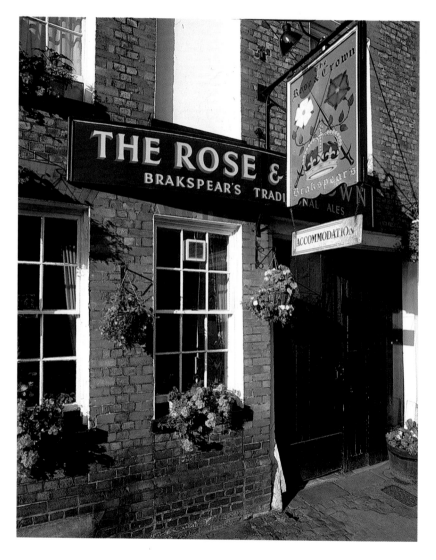

Above The Rose & Crown, Henley-on-Thames

FLOWER POT HOTEL
FERRY LANE, ASTON, HENLEY-ON-THAMES, OXFORDSHIRE

This impressive red-brick Victorian hotel is certainly off the beaten track. From the main road, the narrow lanes that lead to it are full of wild flowers, overgrown in the summer, concealing surrounding fields of barley and wheat. It is only a short stroll to the river. Brakspear's bought the freehold of the original building in 1884, when the ferry was still a going concern, but demolished it in 1890 to make way for the present structure.

As the sign on the exterior states, the hotel provides accommodation for fishing and boating parties, but all visitors are warmly welcomed. It's popular all year round but especially at Regatta time. The lounge bar, with its high Victorian ceiling, has one of the largest collections of stuffed fish in the country. Apparently one is false, but it is difficult to tell, so you can have some fun trying to identify it. The saloon bar provides a less formal atmosphere.

🕑 *11.00-3.00, 6.00-11.00 Mon-Sat; 12.00-3.00, 7.00-10.30 Sun. Occasional all-day opening.*

🍺 *Brakspear Bitter, Mild & Special, Brakspear seasonal beer. Cider: Strongbow.*

🍴 *12.00-2.00 Mon-Sun, 6.30-9.00 Mon-Sat.* Ⓥ

SYMBOLS: 🅿 ❋ 👫 🚃 ❄ 🏠 ➹ 🎡 ⚓

TEL: *01491 574721*

DOG & BADGER
HENLEY ROAD, MEDMENHAM, BUCKINGHAMSHIRE

As soon as you walk into this mediaeval inn, you sense an intriguing past. It was thought to have started life as a church house, where ale would have been brewed for the holy men of St Peter's Church opposite. Even in 1899, the Medmenham parish clerk was still announcing the banns of any forthcoming marriages in the bar of the Dog & Badger before they were issued in church. At one time it was known as the Stag & Huntsman, recalling an era when deer roamed the wild open fields around the river.

Nell Gwynne, lowly orange seller, comic actress and eventually royal mistress, owned a farm nearby and is said to have entertained her admirers at this inn. In fact, along with her regal lover Charles II, she was to visit many inns in her short life, liking the informal atmosphere. During the Civil War, the area around Medmenham was a Royalist stronghold and a Roundhead cannon ball was found embedded in the pub wall when it was being restored.

During the mid 1700s Sir Francis Dashwood founded the Hellfire Club at nearby Medmenham Abbey. He and his Knights of St Francis of Wycombe carried out acts of revolt against Christianity and after a

hard evening of orgies and strange rituals they would retire to the Dog & Badger to discuss their exploits over a quiet drink. Sir Francis was known to like a tipple, and even admitted that while he was Chancellor of the Exchequer he delivered his budget speech to Parliament in a state of intoxication.

🕐 *11.30-3.00, 6.00-11.00 Mon-Sat; 12.00-3.00, 6.00-10.30 Sun. Opens at 5.30 pm in summer.*

🍺 *Brakspear Bitter & Special, occasional guest beer. Cider: Strongbow.*

🍴 *12.00-2.30 Mon-Sun, 7.00-9.30 Mon-Sat.* Ⓥ

SYMBOLS: 🅿 ❄ 🚻 🐕 🔀 🎦

TEL: *01491 571362*

Above Dog & Badger, Medmenham

93

THE BLACK BOY

HENLEY ROAD, HURLEY, BERKSHIRE

A short walk from the river, the exterior of this attractive and brightly coloured 16th-century pub has enticed many travellers off the main road between Henley and Marlow. It acquired its name from that lover of women and good inns, Charles II. Born of a mixed descent consisting of Scottish, Danish, French and Italian blood, he was so dark-skinned from birth that his mother, Henrietta Maria of France, declared that she had borne a black baby.

While Charles was in exile in France, his followers would gather at inns, which took his name: the Black Boy. They were considered safe meeting houses for Royalists where they could discuss at ease their plans to topple Cromwell and return the King to power.

Set at the top of a country lane leading down to the Thames Path, this charming inn provides a welcome haven from the traffic of the main road and hearty well-priced pub food in the bar area.

🕐 *11.30-2.30, 6.00-11.00 Mon-Sat; 12.00-3.00, 7.00-10.30 Sun.*
🛢 *Brakspear Bitter & Mild. Cider: Strongbow.*
🍴 *12.00-2.00 Mon-Sun, 6.30-9.00 Mon-Sat.* ⓥ
SYMBOLS: 🅿 ❄ 👫 🔲 🍽
TEL: *01628 824212*

94

RISING SUN
HIGH STREET, HURLEY, BERKSHIRE

While the sign at the Rising Sun shows a great burning star over rooftops, the origin of the pub's name is not literal. It was originally a heraldic symbol used by Edward III, Richard III, and William of Orange. Here, it is most likely a reference to the latter as deep in the vaults of the Tudor mansion Ladye Place set in Hurley, the local Lovelace family met with other nobles in 1688 to plan the overthrow of James II to install William of Orange in his place. William and his wife, Mary, succeeded to the throne the following year and became joint sovereigns.

As with many small village country inns, its clientele expanded beyond the locals with the advent of the motor car. However, the Reverend F.T.

Wethered of Hurley, having witnessed a horrific accident involving a small boy, resolved to vote only for members of parliament who pledged themselves to abolish 'these damnable engines of Satan, more barbarous than scythed chariots'. Since his plea was unsuccessful, we can now all enjoy the delights of the Rising Sun, a cosy little pub offering great food.

11.30-3.00, 5.30-11.00 Mon-Sat; 12.00-3.00, 7.00-10.30 Sun. Open all day Fri-Sun during permitted hours in summer.
Brakspear Bitter, regular guest beer. Cider: Addlestone, Strongbow.
12.00-2.00 Mon-Sun, 7.00-9.30 Tues-Sat. Ⓥ
SYMBOLS: 🅿 ❄ 👫 🐾 🍽 ⚔ 🏠
TEL: *01628 824274*

THE HOGSHEAD AT MARLOW
82-84 HIGH STREET, MARLOW, BUCKINGHAMSHIRE

One of the youngest pubs on the whole length of the river Thames, the Hogshead was built in the shadow of the Thomas Wethered Brewery. This once-thriving business was established in Marlow in 1758, but it ceased brewing in 1988. The grand old brewhouse, once home to many great beers, including the classic Winter Royal, now houses luxury apartments. Built in 1996, the modern brick exterior of the Hogshead was considered by many locals to be not in keeping with the aged exterior of the other buildings in Marlow High Street.

11.00-11.00 Mon-Sat; 12.00-10.30 Sun.
Abroad Cooper, Boddingtons Bitter, Wadworth 6X, up to 8 regular guest beers, some from local breweries. Cider: cask-conditioned.
11.00-9.00 Mon-Sat; 12.00-9.00 Sun. Ⓥ
SYMBOLS: ❄ ⚔
TEL: *01628 478737*

THE CHEQUERS

51-53 HIGH STREET, MARLOW, BUCKINGHAMSHIRE

This quaint 16th-century inn in the high street of Marlow was constructed from old ships' timbers, said to have been reclaimed from an ocean-going ship shipwrecked off the English coast. It has been in the hands of Brakspear's brewery for over a hundred years. Recent major refurbishment produced two very distinct bars, one traditional in style and the other with a more modern feel.

🏠 *11.00-11.00 Mon-Sat; 12.00-10.30 Sun.*

🍺 *Brakspear Bitter & Special, Brakspear seasonal beer, occasional guest beer. Cider: Strongbow.*

🍴 *12.00-3.00 Mon-Fri; 12-4.00 Sat, Sun; 6.00-9.00 Mon-Thurs.* Ⓥ

SYMBOLS: ❄ 🍴 ↩

TEL: *01628 482053*

THE UNCLE TOM'S CABIN

HILLS LANE, COOKHAM DEANE, BERKSHIRE

The pub started life in the 18th century as two cottages and became a brewery and alehouse about a hundred years later. The chestnut tree at the front, towering over the two-storey structure, is thought to have been planted at the time beer was first served here.

This quiet and unassuming hostelry on Winter Hill overlooks the beech trees of Quarry Wood, thought to have been the inspiration for the Wild Wood of *The Wind in the Willows*.

🏠 *11.00-3.00, 5.30-11.00 Mon-Sat; 12.00-3.00, 7.00-10.30 Sun.*

🍺 *Benskin's Best, Marston's Pedigree, regular guest beer. Cider: Addlestone.*

🍴 *12.00-2.00 (2.30 Sat, Sun), 7.30-10.00 Mon-Sat, 7.30-9.30 Sun.* Ⓥ

SYMBOLS: 🅿 ❄ 🚻 🏠 🏚 🍴

TEL: *01628 483339*

SPADE OAK

COLDMOORHOLME LANE, BOURNE END,
BUCKINGHAMSHIRE

Situated on the very edge of Bourne End, this Victorian inn was built in 1887. It was first referred to as Ye Ferry Hotel, a name that can still be seen on one of the gable ends of the building, when there was a regular ferry to Cockmarsh on the opposite bank at the end of the lane. Presumably the inn changed its name when the ferry stopped operating around 1920.

In the late Victorian and early Edwardian era, the area was very popular with the new leisured classes – boaters, bathers and those just wishing to stroll along the banks of the Thames. Afterwards they would take tea at the hotel, sitting in the grounds in the summer to sample the rural tranquillity. The marshland between Winter Hill and the river has been common land since its charter was granted in 1272, and even today cattle graze in the peace and quiet in the traditional manner.

11.00-11.00 Mon-Sat; 12.00-10.30 Sun.
Brakspear Bitter, Wadworth 6X, 2 changing guest beers. Cider: Strongbow.
11.30-10.00 Mon-Sun. Ⓥ
SYMBOLS: 🅿 ❄ 👬 ⛔ ⛔
TEL: *01628 520090*

THE BOUNTY
THAMES RIVERSIDE, BOURNE END, BUCKS

Accessible only by foot or boat but well worth the expedition. All deliveries are taken across the river by boat. The present building started life as a tea room but developed into an inn when the customers starting demanding something stronger and now the Bounty has a reputation for fine ales and delicious food. There is an old jukebox in the bar and 50p will buy you five plays of the 45 rpm vinyl discs.

12.00-10.30 Mon-Sun (Easter-Sept); 12.00-dusk at weekends all other times of year.

Rebellion Mutiny, 2 changing guest beers. Cider: Strongbow.

12.00-9.00 Mon-Sun. Ⓥ

SYMBOLS: ❄ ⚐ ⌂ ▦ ⚑ ⊞ ⦂

TEL: *01628 520056*

THE OLD SWAN UPPERS
THE POUND, COOKHAM, BERKSHIRE

The 12th-century tradition of swan-upping is an annual census of the swan population taken on certain stretches of the river from Sunbury Lock to Abingdon Bridge. It is carried out in the third week of July by the official Queen's Swan Marker with his fellow Uppers, accompanied by the Swan Uppers of the Vintners' and Dyers' Companies. They row down river to count and check the swan population, marking the cygnets with numbered rings to establish ownership by the Crown, shared with the said livery companies since they were granted the right in the 15th century.

Once called the New Inn, it was renamed in 1982 to its present title. Only a hundred years old, the interior of the building gives the impression of being a lot older, with wonderful flagstone floors, old ships' timbers, exposed brickwork and nicotine-stained paintwork

blending to give a special ambience. If the sun is shining, ask for directions to the pub's secret enclosed garden.

🛏 *11.00-11.00 Mon-Sat; 12.00-10.30 Sun.*

🛢 *Greene King Abbot & IPA. Cider: Scrumpy Jack.*

🍴 *12.00-2.30, 6.30-9.30 Mon-Sun.* Ⓥ

SYMBOLS: 🅿 ❄ 👪 🐾 🔥 💨 🏚

TEL: *01628 521324*

Above The Old Swan Uppers, Cookham

THE CROWN AT COOKHAM
THE MOOR, COOKHAM, BERKSHIRE

This mock-Tudor, ivy-clad building is the third inn to have stood on this site, the last two having been burnt down. When it was last reduced to ashes, in July 1926, the local paper recounted the events of the fateful night. Staying at what was then a hotel, an acrobat called Harold Moxon was roused from his sleep by his bull terrier Dan. Realising that his exit was blocked, he escaped down knotted sheets and then tried, unsuccessfully, to raise the fire brigade. However, the Klofacz brothers, who lived next door, leaped on their motorbike and raced the 3 miles to Maidenhead to get help. By the time it arrived it was too late. With such a history of combustion it's a relief to find the modern fire station where it is – right behind the pub!

The Crown has a marvellous position overlooking Cookham Common, with some wonderful views.

11.00-11.00 Mon-Sat; 12.00-10.30 Sun.
Charles Wells Bombardier, Courage Best, 3 changing guest beers.
Cider: Strongbow.
12.00-2.30 Mon-Fri; 11.00-3.00 Sat; 12.00-3.00 Sun. (V)
Breakfast available daily from 9.30 am.
SYMBOLS: P ✳ ♟ ⌂ ⚫
TEL: *01628 520163*

THE HIND'S HEAD
HIGH STREET, BRAY, BERKSHIRE

The Hind's Head is thought to have been built in the middle of the 16th century, as either a hunting lodge or sleeping quarters for the stonemasons working on the nearby St Michael's Church. During renovation works in 1938 the upstairs walls were found to be made of wattle and daub – a construction method using a network of

Previous pages The Crown at Cookham

rods and twigs plastered with mud or clay. And as further evidence of its age, a Queen Elizabeth I sixpence, minted in 1593, was found in a crack in the floorboards.

The 'Vicar's Room' is reputed to have been the sleeping place for the notorious Vicar of Bray, Simon Alleyn. He was minister of the parish for 48 years in the middle of the 16th century and served the community

throughout the reign of three sovereigns. During the religious upheavals of the time Alleyn managed to keep his position by changing his faith three times! His decision may have been made easier when he witnessed the horrific sight of religious martyrs being burned to death at Windsor. An old English ballad, 'The Vicar of Bray', celebrates his regular conversions. It has been said that his ghost can still be seen in the room where he once slept.

On 23 April 1963, the inn played host to the Queen and Prince Philip, along with foreign royals and dignitaries who had gathered here on the eve of Princess Alexandra's wedding, before the grand ceremony in Westminster Abbey. They dined on saddle of lamb, treacle tart (made to a 15th-century recipe still on the menu today) and Stilton. The men drank English ale, the ladies soft drinks.

These days no accommodation is available, even though the old sign still calls the pub a hotel. The interior is wood panelled, with old beams and high-backed settles. Look out for the wording about the fireplace in the bar – 'Fear Knocked at the door, Faith answered, No one was there.'

Above The Hinds Head, Bray

107

⊞ *11.00-11.00 Mon-Sat; 12.00-3.00, 7.00-10.30 Sun.*
⊞ *Brakspear Special, Courage Best, Fuller's London Pride, occasional guest beer.*
Cider: summer only.
⊞ *12.00-2.30, 7.00-9.30 (9.00 Sun) Mon-Sun.* Ⓥ
SYMBOLS: 🅿 ⚦ ⊞
TEL: *01628 626151*

THE SWAN
MILL LANE, CLEWER VILLAGE, BERKSHIRE

Nobody is quite certain how long an inn has stood on this site, as the parish records in Clewer Church go back only three hundred years. Clewer was a thriving village before William the Conqueror constructed the original Windsor Castle, while parts of the church can be traced back to Saxon times. Buried in the graveyard, a stone's throw from the pub are some of the victims of the Titanic disaster and Sir Daniel Gooch, a regular at the Swan in the later years of his life. At the age of 20 he was made personal assistant to Brunel on the Great Western Railway project, and went on to other ventures such as the Severn Tunnel and the Great Eastern Steamship company.

The Swan, as seen now, was constructed in the 18th century and served the coaches filled with travellers going between Maidenhead and Windsor. Until the 19th century, the inn was also used as the coroner's court, dealing mainly with corpses fished out of the river. The mortuary was sited at the rear, which suited one landlord, Charlie, who was also part-time mortician.

It is still a traditionalists' pub, far away from the tourist trade of Windsor, and has a policy of no music or television.

⊞ *6.00-11.00 Mon-Sat, 12.00-3.00 Sat & Sun only, 7.00-10.30 Sun.*
⊞ *Flowers IPA & Original, Fuller's London Pride. Cider: Scrumpy Jack.*
SYMBOLS: 🅿 ❄ ⚦ ⊞ ⏎ 🍺
TEL: *01753 862069*

THE NEW COLLEGE

55 HIGH STREET, ETON, WINDSOR, BERKSHIRE

The College Arms, as it used be known, was rebuilt in the 1930s in a neo-Georgian style, presenting a wonderful façade to all those walking the Eton high street pathways. It took its present name in 1998, when it was refitted in the Victorian style with decorative half-glazed wooden screens, high-backed settles, period light fittings and black and white prints of the locality. A perfect example of how an old pub, tarnished with age and use, can be properly refurbished. The wonderful Badger beers and traditional English cuisine create a perfect harmony.

11.00-11.00 Mon-Sat; 12.00-10.30 Sun.
Badger IPA, Dorset Best, Roberts Pride, Tanglefoot. Cider: Blackthorn.
12.00-9.30 Mon-Sun. ⓥ
SYMBOLS: ❄ ⛄ 🐾 ⚑
TEL: *01753 865516*

THE WATERMANS ARMS

BROCAS STREET, ETON, WINDSOR, BERKSHIRE

Built around 1542, this deceptively large building had a multitude of uses in its time. In 1665 London was struck by the Great Plague, taking lives indiscriminately and eventually killing over a hundred thousand people. When the plague reached Windsor and the surrounding districts, this pub was commandeered as a makeshift mortuary to cope with the huge number of bodies. The ghosts sometimes heard walking around the rooms are thought to be victims of this terrible tragedy.

Above The New College, Eton

By 1682 it was the private residence of the brewer Robert Style, even though there were no plans to convert it into a beerhouse. It remained in private hands until 1793, when the then owner, Stephen Boult, a coachmaker, was declared bankrupt and the building was sold to the parish for £485 for use as a workhouse. The workhouse did not last long, and in the early-19th century the building opened its doors to the public as a hostelry.

Located off Eton high street and hidden from the river, the effort to seek it out is made easier by the colourful exterior. The large conservatory dining area has a tree growing through the roof.

🍴 *11.00-2.30 Mon-Thurs; 11.00-3.00 Fri, Sat; 12.00-3.00 Sun; 6.00-11.00 Mon-Sat; 7.00-10.30 Sun.*

🍺 *Brakspear Best, Charles Wells Bombardier, Courage Best & Directors, Greene King IPA, John Smith's, Wadworth 6X. Cider: Scrumpy Jack.*

🍽 *12.00-2.00 Mon-Sun, 6.00-8.45 Mon-Sat.* ⓥ

SYMBOLS: 👥 🍴 🏠 🌙 🍽

TEL: *01753 861001*

THE FORT & FIRKIN
THE PROMENADE, BARRY AVENUE, WINDSOR, BERKSHIRE

Once called the Thames Hotel, this large pub by the river has been well and truly 'firkinised', with bare floorboards, brewery memorabilia and a minimum amount of furniture. Although in the spit-and-sawdust style, it is a popular venue and can get very busy, especially in the summer months.

🍴 *11.00-11.00 Mon-Sat; 12.00-10.30 Sun.*

🍺 *Firkin Best, Dogbolter & Fort. Cider: Stowford Press, Weston's Scrumpy.*

🍽 *12.00-8.00 Mon-Sat; 12.00-7.00 Sun.* ⓥ

SYMBOLS: ❄ 🍴 🏠 🌙 🍽

TEL: *01753 869897*

THE ROYAL OAK
DATCHET ROAD, WINDSOR, BERKSHIRE

The name the Royal Oak, one of the most popular in England, has patriotic links to Charles II. After his defeat at the Battle of Worcester in 1651 he escaped with his trusty companion, Colonel Carless. They hid from the Roundheads from noon until dusk in the mighty Boscobel Oak Tree in Salop. When Charles was eventually returned to the throne it was proclaimed that 29 May, the King's birthday, would henceforth be celebrated as Royal Oak Day.

More than seventy years later, in 1727, Thomas Skinner became the first landlord of the Royal Oak. His licence was one of 41 granted at the Brewster sessions in the Guildhall at Windsor, so it seems that competition in those days was quite rife. The licensee from 1869 to 1880, Thomas Pennicott, was the uncle of H.G. Wells.

The mock-Elizabethan structure now standing in the shadow of Windsor Castle was probably built at some time after the Second World War.

⊞ *11.00-11.00 Mon-Sat; 12.00-10.30 Sun.*

▦ *Courage Best & Directors, Wadworth 6X, occasional guest beer. Cider: Scrumpy Jack, Blackthorn.*

⊞ *11.00-10.00 Mon-Sat; 12.00-10.00 Sun.* ⓥ

SYMBOLS: ❋ ♳ ▦ ▣ ⊠

TEL: *01753 865179*

THE DONKEY HOUSE
10 THAMESIDE, WINDSOR, BERKSHIRE

T ake the time and trouble to seek out this inn, positioned by the river in one of the nicest and quietest spots in this busy royal town.

It was originally known as the King's Arms, but was altered in 1953 to the Donkey House. The nickname was a tribute to the bargees who travelled the river in the days of commercial freight, who would often stop at this tavern to stable their horses and donkeys. While the animals were resting the men would drink and make merry, swapping tales of the river.

It underwent a major refit in early 1999 providing this large pub with facilities to welcome all visitors.

🛏 *11.00-11.00 Mon-Sat; 12.00-10.30 Sun.*
🍺 *Marston's Pedigree, Morland Old Speckled Hen, Tetley Bitter, regular guest beer. Cider: Blackthorn.*
🍴 *12.00-9.00 Mon-Fri; 12.00-7.00 Sat, Sun.* Ⓥ
SYMBOLS: ❄ 👫 🛏 🔌
TEL: *01753 860644*

DATCHET
TO
WALTON-
ON-THAMES

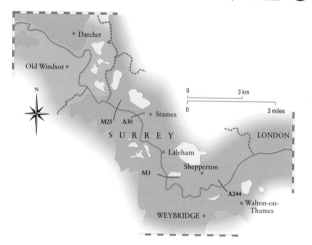

Although only a stone's throw from its neighbour, Royal Windsor, Datchet is often overlooked by the tourists. It has a green, some fine pubs, historic houses, and was even mentioned in Shakespeare's The Merry Wives of Windsor.

The astronomer Sir William Herschel, who discovered Uranus in 1781, lived in Datchet with his sister Caroline for three years at the end of the 18th century. Herschel was also a skilled telescope maker, and constructed what was then the world's largest telescope at Slough with a focal length of 40 feet.

From Datchet the Thames passes under Albert Bridge, which was named for the Prince Consort, who recommended the building of two identical bridges at opposite ends of the town after the one and only crossing kept falling down.

Soon the river reaches Old Windsor. From the name you would expect a village that has stood the test of time, but in fact the majority of houses here have not even celebrated their first centenary. Evidently it obtained its name from the 9th-century village that grew up around a Saxon royal palace. The tomb of Mary Robinson, an actress well-known in the 18th century, lies in the churchyard of St Peter & St Andrew. Having seen her performance as Perdita in Shakespeare's *The Winter's Tale*, the Prince of Wales, later George IV, chose her as his mistress. After he tired of her she was left to a life of poverty and died at the early age of 42.

The river then enters the tranquil location of Runnymede, spoiled only by the road that runs parallel to the river. Here you will find the monument to the signing of the Magna Carta in 1215, although exactly where in Runnymede the document was actually signed is not known.

The Thames passes under one of the busiest sections of London's orbital motorway, the M25, before entering Staines. It is a very busy town and the old and new buildings mingle with neither dominating. The stone bridge at Staines has survived since 1832, but in the fifty years that preceded this date four other bridges had to be demolished. Firstly, due to old age, the mediaeval bridge had to go; secondly, the timber replacement cracked, forcing it to be demolished; thirdly, an iron structure failed miserably; finally, the attempt in a combination of wood and iron was also unsuccessful.

Leaving suburban Staines, the river soon flows past Penton Hook, where a sharp U-bend hides the entrance to a large marina. Those

Above The Swan Hotel, Staines

travelling by boat have the option of using the bypass running past Penton Lock.

Onwards, the river reaches Laleham where the village ignores the mighty Thames. Its most famous resident was Thomas Arnold, the headmaster of Rugby School and reformer of the public school system. There is an account of him in Thomas Hughes' *Tom Brown's Schooldays*. Arnold's son Matthew, the 19th-century poet and critic, was born in Laleham and is buried in the grounds of All Saints Church.

Past Laleham Abbey, the former home of the Lucan family (though not the famous missing earl), the river flows through Chertsey on its way to Shepperton Lock. If you fancy a trip across the water, a ferry takes passengers to the Weybridge side, providing a link with the shortest route on the towpath. This is the Desborough Cut, which was finished in 1935. It was named after the longest-serving chairman of the Thames Conservancy, Lord Desborough, who was a great sportsman and twice swam across the pool beneath the Niagara Falls – he performed the feat for a second time to convince people that he had succeeded the first time!

If you decide to go the long way round you are rewarded by the old village of Shepperton, where you will find a square, some pubs, a church, a rectory and old houses. One frequent visitor to the rectory during the mid-18th century was J.M. Neale, who spoke 24 languages and wrote 136 hymns, including 'Good King Wenceslas'.

Whichever route you take, you will come to the town of Walton-on-Thames, which has a number of good pubs by the river.

MORNING STAR
THE GREEN, DATCHET, BERKSHIRE

This fine village pub, set in a listed building, provides a friendly atmosphere in which to enjoy some good food and drink. Nothing pretentious will be found here as the wooden floors, furniture and old stone fireplace prove. In the main bar are artefacts relating to the astronomer, Sir William Herschel who lived in the village for a short period during his life. In the back bar there is an open skylight so the stars can be enjoyed, but unfortunately not the Morning Star as this only appears shortly before sunrise.

11.00-11.00 Mon-Sat; 12.00-10.30 Sun.
Ushers Best & Founders Ale. Cider: Scrumpy Jack.
12.00-2.30, 7.00-9.30 Mon-Sat; 12.00-6.00 Sun. Ⓥ
SYMBOLS: 🅿 ❄ 👫 🏠
TEL: *01753 591399*

THE ROYAL STAG
THE GREEN, DATCHET, BERKSHIRE

Originally a coaching inn by the turnpike on the London to Windsor route, this pub started life as the Five Bells, became the High Flyer, and eventually changed to its present name in the mid-1850s.

It has been extensively modernised over the years, the eastern wall facing the churchyard is still the original Elizabethan structure, retaining the black beams, white walls and old windows. A child's handprint has appeared on one of the small panes of glass many times over the years. Among the many stories of whose it might be, this one seems to have most credence. In the middle of winter a labourer, accompanied by his young son, was making his way home after a hard day's work. He stopped at the inn to take refreshment in the company of his friends, leaving the boy outside to play in the heavy snow. When the child became very wet and cold, he tried to gain the attention of his father by calling out and knocking on the window but it was now so noisy inside the inn that his cries went unnoticed. His body was discovered later against the church wall. In 1979 the glass was removed for examination, but showed no traces – although the mark did appear on the new pane that had replaced it.

🕐 *11.00-11.00 Mon-Sat; 12.00-10.30 Sun.*
🍺 *Burton Ale, Marston's Pedigree, Tetley Bitter, regular guest beer.*
Cider: Blackthorn.
🍴 *12.00-2.00 Mon-Sun, 6.00-8.45 Mon-Sat.* ⓥ
SYMBOLS: 🅿 🐕 🏨 🎹
TEL: *01753 548218*

Above The Royal Stag, Datchet

THE LORD NELSON
4 DATCHET ROAD, OLD WINDSOR, BERKSHIRE

A pub on this site can be traced back to the reign of George III. It stands opposite one of the many back doors leading into the Windsor Castle estate, and the occasional royal may be spotted entering or leaving by car. The Lord Nelson, and the land on which it stands, is owned by the Crown.

12.00-11.00 Mon-Sat; 12.00-10.30 Sun.
Morland Original, Ruddles Best, regular guest beer in summer.
Cider: Blackthorn.
12.00-2.30 Mon-Sun. Ⓥ
SYMBOLS: 🅿 ❄ 👥
TEL: *01753 858746*

BLUE ANCHOR
13-15 HIGH STREET, STAINES, MIDDLESEX

A n imposing three-storey building, the Blue Anchor is over five hundred years old. It would once have been an important coaching inn serving visitors to the town.

The Georgian frontage was added in 1700, a combination of exquisite brickwork and sash windows, although five of them are false. When the window tax was introduced in 1789 it became common practice to brick up those that weren't needed. When the law was repealed in 1851 no one bothered to reopen them, but instead painted them to resemble frames and curtains.

It was thought to have been called the Blue Anchor to avoid any confusion with the Crown & Anchor once located in the high street, which was demolished in 1957. During that same year, while refurbishment works were being carried out at this pub, an oak beam forming the main support was uncovered and was estimated to be over

six hundred and fifty years old. When the floor in one of the upstairs bedrooms was being worked on during this same period, they found another complete floor underneath with the date of 1498 marked on one of the wooden boards.

Staines Market, which dates back even further than the pub, is held on Wednesdays and Saturdays in the town hall nearby. You could browse for a bargain before adjourning to the Blue Anchor for a cup of tea or coffee, some good pub grub or just for a drink.

🕑 *11.00-11.00 Mon-Sat; 12.00-10.30 Sun.*

🍺 *Boddingtons Bitter, Courage Best, Marston's Pedigree, Morland Old Speckled Hen, Wadworth 6X, occasional guest beer. Cider: Strongbow.*

🍴 *10.00-9.00 Mon-Sat; 12.00-9.00 Sun.* Ⓥ

Breakfast available daily except Sun from 10.00 am.

SYMBOLS: 🅿 ❄ ✜

TEL: *01784 469426*

Above The Swan Hotel, Staines

THE SWAN HOTEL
THE HYTHE, STAINES, MIDDLESEX

Although often cited as being in Staines, technically this fine inn stands in Egham Hythe on the south bank of the river, near the bridge. The first recorded mention of the Swan was as far back as 1606, but the present building is 18th century with obvious later additions.

It was once the haunt of bargees transporting their cargoes on the river. The custom was for the inn to issue tokens to these men instead of change, thereby ensuring their return. The tokens are now collectors' items, though the present landlord is unlikely to accept them behind the bar.

Between 1659 and 1662 Samuel Pepys noted in his diary that he visited the Swan Tavern. After a meal here he would travel back to Westminster by boat, a distance of 40 miles, which by rowing boat would have taken a considerable time.

The hotel offers a wonderful position by the river from which to watch the graceful swans and passing boaters. If you happen to be in town during the third week in July you may be lucky enough to see the Swan Uppers mooring alongside for refreshment.

11.00-11.00 Mon-Sat; 12.00-10.30 Sun.
Fuller's Chiswick Bitter, ESB & London Pride, Fuller's seasonal beer. Cider: Scrumpy Jack.
12.00-10.00 Mon-Sat; 12.00-9.30 Sun. Ⓥ
SYMBOLS: ❄ 👫 🐕 🍴 🍺 🚪 🔌
TEL: *01784 452494*

THE JOLLY FARMER
THE HYTHE, STAINES, MIDDLESEX

For well over three hundred years this friendly inn has been a favourite meeting place for fisherman to swap stories of the size of the one that got away. Perhaps it should have been called the Jolly Fisherman instead.

An interesting feature is the names inscribed on one of the saloon bar windows. Legend says they are the signatures of young men who called here before setting off to the Boer War. However, according to a local man, Arthur Bedford, his brother George cut the pane of glass in 1904. At the time there were five Bedford men drinking at the bar: George, his father Jim, another brother and two cousins. Arthur, only ten at the time, was not allowed in the bar and had to stand by the door. George had always boasted what an expert glass cutter he was and demonstrated his skills by etching all their names on the window.

🔲 *11.00-11.00 Mon-Sat; 12.00-10.30 Sun.*
🍺 *Ushers Best, Founders Ale. Cider: Blackthorn.*
🍽 *12.00-2.15 Mon-Sun, 6.00-9.30 Tues-Sat.* Ⓥ
SYMBOLS: ❄ 👥 🍽
TEL: *01784 452807*

THE WHEATSHEAF & PIGEON
PENTON ROAD, STAINES, MIDDLESEX

This is the only pub with this name in the country. While the wheatsheaf can be linked to Penton's agricultural background, there is no known reason for the inclusion of the pigeon. Perhaps at one time pigeons were prevalent in the area, or they might have been on the menu.

A photograph in the bar records a time when the Thames flooded over a hundred yards from the riverbank, reaching the pub and surrounding area. One man, not wishing to miss his daily pint, donned his waterproofs and set off in his punt. He successfully navigated his way to his favourite watering hole and was able to park his boat in the bar.

It could perhaps be described as a back-street local, but this would not be doing it justice because it is a truly excellent pub that must be visited to appreciate all its many qualities. Meat lovers should try the massive mixed grill!

⊞ *11.00-11.00 Mon-Sat; 12.00-10.30 Sun.*

▣ *Courage Best & Directors, regular guest beer. Cider: Scrumpy Jack, Strongbow.*

⊞ *12.00-2.00, 6.00-9.30 Mon-Sat; 12.00-9.00 Sun.* Ⓥ

SYMBOLS: 🅿 ❊ ♟

TEL: *01784 452922*

THE THREE HORSESHOES AT LALEHAM
SHEPPERTON ROAD, LALEHAM, MIDDLESEX

Parts of this picturesque old building can be traced back to the 16th century. At various times it has served as a coaching inn, police station, morgue, coroner's court and hunting lodge. The earliest recorded mention of there being an inn here was in 1624, and by 1726 it was called the Horseshoes or simply the Shoes. It gained the Three in the title some twenty years later.

Perhaps its best-known landlord was William Clifton. While he was host, from 1884 until 1925, many famous people passed through the doors. Sir Arthur Sullivan, creator with William Gilbert of many fine operas, helped out behind the bar one busy bank holiday. Another who also graced the Three Horseshoes with his presence was King Edward VII, who would often visit when calling on the Earl of Lucan at Laleham Abbey. His Majesty would take his tipple in the bar parlour (now the King's room), which Bill Clifton reserved for his inner circle and the odd illustrious guest. An invitation to join whoever was in the parlour was a sign of having climbed to the top of Laleham's social ladder. Anyone visiting this popular pub can now sit wherever they choose.

🕎 *11.00-11.00 Mon-Sat; 12.00-10.30 Sun.*
🍺 *Courage Best, Fuller's London Pride, 3 guest beers. Cider: Strongbow.*
🍽 *12.00-2.30 Mon-Sun, 6.00-9.00 Mon-Sat; 12.00-9.30 Sat, 12.00-8.30 Sun in summer.* ⓥ
SYMBOLS: 🅿 ❄ 🚻 🏠 ❎ 🍽
TEL: *01784 452617*

THAMES COURT
TOWPATH, SHEPPERTON, MIDDLESEX

This large, imposing building near Shepperton Lock was built as the private residence for the Dutch Ambassador early in the 20th century. This had some influence on the interior décor, such as hand-painted Delft tiling, oak panelling and beautiful fireplaces, some of which remain to this day. It remained as a dwelling house until the 1950s, when it became a guesthouse with a select private members club known as Thames Court.

In the front garden is an Indian bean tree, with branches growing in every direction, which towers above the building and dominates the scene. Around June and July it bears pencil-thick cylindrical pods about 35cm long. The large outdoor seating area here becomes a perfect amphitheatre on a summer's day, with the Thames providing a constantly changing performance.

The massive interior was tastefully refurbished in 1997, providing flagstone floors, old beams and exposed brick walls, all combining to give a layout resembling a labyrinth.

🏛 *11.00-11.00 Mon-Sat; 12.00-10.30 Sun.*
🛢 *Bass, Fuller's London Pride. Cider: Blackthorn.*
🍴 *12.00-10.00 Mon-Sat; 12.00-9.30 Sun.* Ⓥ
SYMBOLS: 🅿 ❄ 👫 🐕 🔥 ⚒
TEL: *01932 221957*

Above Thames Court, Shepperton

THE OLD CROWN

83 THAMES STREET, WEYBRIDGE, SURREY

This traditional inn, sited on the southern banks of the Thames, near the gateway to the Wey Navigation Canal, was probably built during the 17th century. Its first licence is recorded as having been issued in 1729, so it deserves the 'Old' added to the Crown, the name by which it started life. It was once a favourite stopping place for bargees using Weybridge Wharf; their sleeping quarters were in what is now the lounge bar.

The pub has been in the care of the same family for over forty years. The external white weatherboarding makes it stand out in all weathers, and in sunlight it positively shines like a beacon. This style of cladding was once common in the surrounding district, but very few examples now remain.

At one time the pub had five bars, though this has now been reduced to three, and a conservatory was added recently.

10.30-11.00 Mon-Sat; 12.00-3.00, 7.00-10.30 Sun.

Courage Best & Directors, 2 regular guest beers. Cider: Blackthorn, Scrumpy Jack.

12.00-2.00 (2.30 Sat) Mon-Sun, 7.00-9.00 Mon-Sat. Ⓥ

SYMBOLS: P

TEL: *01932 842844*

THE LINCOLN ARMS
104 THAMES STREET, WEYBRIDGE, SURREY

This grand building started life as two cottages. During the reign of Henry VIII, the then Earl of Lincoln was so highly favoured by His Majesty that he was rewarded with these dwellings, which formed the entrance to the Earl's estate, Oatlands Park. They remained under the control of the family until the 18th century. There are no records of when it became a pub, but it is certainly one of Weybridge's oldest inns. It took several names, including the Anchor and the Row Barge, before it became the Lincoln Arms.

Its large, modern and bright interior makes it a popular pub for customers of all ages.

▥ *12.00-11.00 Mon-Sat; 12.00-10.30 Sun.*
▧ *Marston's Pedigree, Morland Old Speckled Hen, Tetley Bitter, occasional guest beer. Cider: Blackthorn.*
▨ *12.00-3.00 Mon-Sun, 7.00-10.00 Mon-Sat.* Ⓥ
SYMBOLS: 🅿 ✳ ♂♀ ▦ ◨ ◩ ◪
TEL: *01932 842109*

THE KING'S HEAD
CHURCH SQUARE, SHEPPERTON, MIDDLESEX

Sited in Church Square – part of old Shepperton, where no modern buildings seem to exist – parts of this quaint and cosy old coaching inn are said to be nearly five hundred years old. The sign outside portrays the head of Charles I, though legend dictates that it was his son Charles II and his lover Nell Gwynne who used to stop here on their way to Windsor.

During the 18th century it became famous for society tea parties so the beer glasses were put away and replaced with the finest bone china. On their arrival by horse and carriage, the local gentry would enter the

King's Head for a cup of Earl Grey or Darjeeling, with smoked salmon sandwiches and fine cakes. Where the regulars were going for a drink while this was going on no one knows.

During one of the two periods when they were married to each other, Elizabeth Taylor and Richard Burton were filming at nearby Shepperton Studios and used this pub as their local. It is said they once staged a sausage roll fight in the bar. These days the food is served in a more sedate manner. The pub has some outstanding internal features such as the old brick inglenook fireplace, worn flagstone floors and panelled walls which have stood the test of time.

🕒 *11.00-11.00 Mon-Sat; 12.00-10.30 Sun.*
🍺 *Courage Best, Theakston Best, regular guest beer. Cider: Blackthorn.*
🍽 *12.00-2.15 Mon-Sat, 7.00-9.45 Mon-Thur.* Ⓥ
SYMBOLS: ❄ 👫 🕒
TEL: *01932 221910*

THE RED LION
RUSSELL ROAD, SHEPPERTON, MIDDLESEX

During his reign, King James I ordered that the sign of the red lion, a heraldic tribute to Scotland, be displayed in public places. As this inn is reported to have been built in the 17th century, it seems probable that this is how the name was acquired.

The exterior of the building is covered from ground to roof in wisteria that provides a colourful decoration when it flowers in May/June. There is an outside seating area at the front of the pub and also, on the north bank of the river, an enclosed beer garden but you have to cross the main Shepperton to Walton road between it and the bar.

Inside is a wealth of oak panelling and the customary old beams which add to the atmosphere of this excellent inn. Above the bar you will find

the characters YCHJCY10PFOCB, but you will have to visit in person and part with some money to find out what it means.

 *11.00-11.00 Mon-Sat; 12.00-10.30 Sun.*

 *Courage Best & Directors, Fuller's London Pride, occasional guest beer. Cider: Blackthorn.*

 *12.00-2.30, 5.30-9.30 Mon-Fri; 12.00-9.30 Sat; 12.00-8.30 Sun.*

SYMBOLS:

TEL: *01932 244526*

THE OLD MANOR INN

113 MANOR ROAD, WALTON-ON-THAMES, SURREY

With a name like the Old Manor Inn, you know there must be a manor house close by. In this case it's right behind the pub. The 500-year-old timber-framed house built for Walton Leigh was once the lodgings of John Bradshaw, president of the court that condemned Charles I to death in January 1649.

The inn itself is thought to be only 190 years old, with the first licence being granted in 1866 to a local fisherman, John Rosewell. Parts of a silent 1915 film of Dickens' *Barnaby Rudge* were filmed in a little alley next door.

The pub's plain exterior does not do justice to the wonderful welcome you will receive when you step inside the bar. It may be small but it's big on atmosphere.

▣ *11.00-3.00, 5.30-11.00 Mon-Fri; 11.00-11.00 Sat; 12.00-4.00, 7.00-10.30 Sun.*

▣ *Courage Best, Marston's Pedigree, occasional guest beer. Cider: Strongbow.*

▣ *12.00-2.00 Mon-Sun.* Ⓥ

SYMBOLS: ✳ ⌷ *(Lunch only)* ▦ ▣ ⌷

TEL: *01932 221359*

THE SWAN

50 MANOR ROAD, WALTON-ON-THAMES, SURREY

There has been an inn on this site since 1769, though the present building dates only from the late 1870s. It's one of the many pubs on the river that derives its name from the annual ceremony of Swan Upping carried out in July. It's very popular with all users of the river and towpath throughout the year.

The composer of 'Ol' Man River' and 'Smoke Gets in Your Eyes', Jerome Kern, stopped at what was then the Swan Hotel in 1910 while

enjoying a trip along the Thames. On entering the bar, Kern set eyes on the licensee's daughter, Eva Leale. It was a case of love at first sight, which resulted in their marriage and a happy association that would last until Kern's death in 1945.

This is one of only a handful of pubs left in south-east England that can still boast a public bar where beer is sold at a cheaper price than in the other two bars. But the same distinctive Young's beers are there to be sampled in all three drinking areas.

11.00-11.00 Mon-Sat; 12.00-10.30 Sun.

Young's Bitter & Special, Young's seasonal beer. Cider: Blackthorn.

12.00-2.30, 7.00-9.30 Mon-Sun. ⓥ

SYMBOLS: 🅿 ❊ 🚹 🐕 ▥ ⛽ 🍽 ☺

TEL: 01932 225964

THE WEIR

TOWPATH, WATERSIDE DRIVE, WALTON-ON-THAMES, SURREY

A pub that stood on this glorious site near Sunbury Weir was known as the New Inn until 1875, when it was renamed the Weir Hotel. In 1904 it was burned to the ground, perhaps because, at the time, the Walton fire brigade had only antiquated hand pumps, which, given the amount of water close by, must have been frustrating for the firemen. During the same year, there were another three serious fires in Walton which helped fuel the campaign for a new steam-driven fire engine.

Out of the ashes rose the grand Edwardian building we see today, an imposing landmark standing tall over the Thames. During its time as a hotel, which ended in 1994, there would have been many fine functions held at this location, away from the hustle and bustle of everyday life.

11.00-11.00 Mon-Sat; 12.00-10.30 Sun.
Badger Dorset Best & Tanglefoot. Cider: Blackthorn.
11.00-10.00 Mon-Sat; 12.00-9.30 Sun. Ⓥ
SYMBOLS: 🅿 ❄ 🚻 🛏 ✂ ⌕
TEL: *01932 782078*

SUNBURY-
ON-THAMES
TO
TWICKENHAM

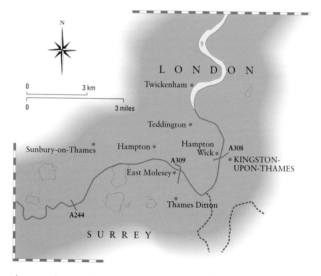

Sunbury, along with a number of other locations on the river,
combines the ancient and modern; fortunately though, the old
village can be found next to the Thames.

A gentle stroll round the village will reveal the 'quasi-Byzantine' church of St Mary the Virgin and no shortage of pubs. Within the churchyard an old yew tree stands, said to be the one in Dickens' *Oliver Twist* where the rogue Bill Sykes and young Oliver heard the clock strike seven on their way to the Shepperton robbery.

You will want to hurry along the next section, unless you are a lover of reservoirs and waterworks, but the beauty is restored when the village of Hampton is reached, which is separated from the north bank of the river by the main road to Hampton Court. In 1754 the innovative actor David Garrick bought Hampton House, which is connected by an underground tunnel to Garrick's Temple, designed by Capability Brown to house Roubiliac's statue of Shakespeare (now housed in the British Museum in London). Dr Samuel Johnson, a long-time friend of the actor, was a regular visitor and came to love Hampton.

The road runs alongside the boundary of Bushy Park, part of the magnificent grounds of Hampton Court where, if you are lucky, you will be able to see the royal deer roaming freely, now safe from the hunters of yesteryear. Very soon Hampton Court Palace in all its glory comes into view. It was originally built by Cardinal Wolsey in 1514, at the time one of the richest men in England, who gave it to Henry VIII as a gesture of goodwill. The king set about making a grand house into an even grander royal palace, now a venue not to be missed.

Across the water lies East Molesey, often overlooked in favour of its grander neighbour, though its shops, pubs and restaurants can be quite a relief if you wish to escape the many visitors to Hampton Court. The opening of the railway in 1840 doubled the population within a decade.

The river flows on, flanked by Hampton Court Park on one side and the village of Thames Ditton on the other. It was reported that when Charles I escaped from house arrest at the palace on the evening of 11 November 1647, he used a wherry to cross the river. He landed on the south bank at Thames Ditton and from there proceeded on foot.

From Surbiton the river soon enters the Royal Borough of Kingston-upon-Thames, where seven Saxon kings were crowned. Now a large

Above The Boaters Inn, Kingston-upon-Thames

shopping centre, the town itself has become a developer's dream and new buildings have sprung up where you might have thought it was impossible to build. Hidden amongst all the glittering glass and steel are still some wonderful monuments from the town's past such as the Market House and the Lovekyn Chapel of St Mary Magdelene.

Heading northwards, the Thames soon encounters the private houses and flats built beside the river, experiencing its last non-tidal stages before reaching Teddington Lock. Noël Coward, one of the truly great Englishmen of the 20th century, was born in Teddington in 1899. Another resident, R.D. Blackmore, the author of *Lorna Doone*, was asked to be godfather to young Master Coward. He refused, though, because his brother Russell, for whom he had acted as godparent, had died at the age of six and Blackmore thought he had brought bad luck to the family. The famous television studios are also near here.

From here the river is tidal and becomes a grand waterway with no more locks to hinder its journey. It passes Strawberry Hill on the left, where the novelist and politician Horace Walpole converted his house into a Gothic monument.

Twickenham (or Twiccas', as it is sometimes known) soon comes into view. Alexander Pope, the witty poet, lived here from 1719. The house no longer stands but part of his famous grotto connecting the two gardens still remains. The grotto, adorned with shells and rock crystals illuminated naturally by light from mirrors, was the inspiration for several of Pope's great poems. The riverside here is the perfect place for a gentle stroll, perhaps after a delicious lunch or dinner. Eel Pie Island, named after the dish that used to be served there, can be accessed by bridge from the embankment. The island became notorious in the 1960s when groups such as The Rolling Stones and The Who stayed in its hotel. The hotel closed some years later and now virtually all the buildings on the island are private dwellings.

THE FLOWER POT

THAMES STREET, SUNBURY-ON-THAMES, MIDDLESEX

We must look back to the Civil War to discover the origin of the name of this old tavern. Before then it may have been called the Inn of Annunciation, with the sign consisting of the Virgin Mary, the baby Jesus and the Archangel Gabriel set by a bunch of lilies, a symbol of purity. This was fine until Oliver Cromwell came to power in the mid-17th century when, with the help of Puritan soldiers, all references to the Catholic religion were obliterated. To comply, the three characters were removed and a flower pot added to contain the lilies.

In 1714 the waterman Thomas Winnall bequeathed the inn to his wife. It seems that at that time it was actually sited across the road, though sometime between 1743 and 1748 it was moved to the present position. When the road at the front was the main thoroughfare to London, it is thought that during the days of the tyre tax this may have been the last stopping point, where wheels were changed.

The exterior retains many of the original features such as the columns supporting the first floor balcony, but as with so many things, age can sometimes take a toll on its beauty. This true free house offers a generous selection of cask-conditioned ales in a traditional setting.

⊞ *11.00-11.00 Mon-Sat; 12.00-10.30 Sun.*
⊞ *Bass, Brakspear Bitter, Greene King Abbot & IPA, regular guest beer. Cider: Addlestone, Strongbow.*
⊞ *12.00-9.30 Mon-Sat; 12.00-4.00 Sun.* ⓥ
SYMBOLS: 🅿 🚻 ⬛ 🔲 🍴
TEL: *01932 780741*

THE MAGPIE
64 THAMES STREET, SUNBURY-ON-THAMES, MIDDLESEX

The name of this 19th-century riverside inn refers not to the bird, but to a half-pint measure, which was once commonly known as a magpie. It was originally a hotel to cater for the many visitors to the river in early Victorian times and still serves its customers well.

▪ *11.00-11.00 Mon-Sat; 12.00-10.30 Sun.*
▪ *Greene King Abbot & IPA, 2 regular guest beers. Cider: Strongbow.*
▪ *12.00-2.30, 6.00-9.00 Mon-Sun.* Ⓥ
SYMBOLS: ❄ 👥 🏠 🗲 🐕
TEL: *01932 782024*

THE JOLLY COOPERS
16 HIGH STREET, HAMPTON, MIDDLESEX

A marvellous 18th-century inn, often overlooked by visitors to the village of Hampton. The present building was first used as a glass and ale house in 1727, where the vagrants of the village would gather to drink before being thrown out at closing time. Servants from Hampton Court Palace would also often use this drinking establishment when the other nearby taverns were full.

There is a list of all the landlords from when the pub opened to the present day in the bar. The present incumbent of this excellent free house has held the post for over a decade but his enthusiasm has not dwindled.

▪ *11.00-3.00, 5.00-11.00 Mon-Fri; 11.00-11.00 Sat; 12.00-10.30 Sun.*
▪ *Courage Best, Fuller's London Pride, Young's Bitter, 2 regular guest beers. Cider: Blackthorn.*
▪ *11.00-2.30 Mon-Sat; 7.00-9.30 Tues-Sat; 12.30-3.30 Sun.* Ⓥ
SYMBOLS: 🅿 ❄ 👥 🚲 🏠 🗲 🍽
TEL: *020 8979 3384*

THE BELL INN

8 THAMES STREET, HAMPTON, MIDDLESEX

This lofty building, with its majestic exterior, was erected at the end of the 19th century, though there has been an inn on the site since the beginning of the 16th century. The old Bell Hotel was destroyed by fire in 1892.

Dr Johnson described the inn as being neat and clean. He must have visited when calling on his close friend David Garrick, who lived at Hampton House. It's still spick and span but now has a modern interior, with pine tables, leather chesterfield sofas and contemporary furnishings.

🛏 *11.00-11.00 Mon-Sat; 12.00-10.30 Sun.*

🍺 *Adnams Best, Fuller's London Pride, Greene King IPA, Young's Bitter. Cider: Blackthorn, Scrumpy Jack.*

🍴 *12.00-3.00, 6.30-9.30 Mon-Sun.* Ⓥ

SYMBOLS: 🅿 ❄ 🚻 🛏

TEL: *020 8941 9799*

THE PRINCE OF WALES
23 BRIDGE ROAD, EAST MOLESEY, SURREY

This large Victorian building was constructed as a hotel in 1840, which coincided with the opening of the railway line to Hampton Court. It probably didn't start life as the Prince of Wales as most pubs with this name refer to Queen Victoria's eldest son, who wasn't born until 1841. It is very much an old coaching inn and the stables where horses rested were still intact until recently. They were demolished to make way for the restaurant.

In the large interior there is a gallery of pictures depicting Princes of Wales down the years.

12.00-11.00 Mon-Sat; 12.00-10.30 Sun.
Greene King Abbot & IPA, regular guest beer. Cider: Strongbow.
12.00-9.00 Mon-Sat; 12.00-6.00 Sun. Ⓥ
SYMBOLS: 🅿 ❄ 🚻 📷
TEL: *020 8979 5561*

THE KING'S ARMS
LION GATE, HAMPTON COURT ROAD, EAST MOLESEY, SURREY

This great hostelry is to be found next to the Lion Gate entrance to Hampton Court Palace. The site was first mentioned in the manor book of 1658 when two widowed sisters, Mary Spurling and Mary Johnson, were granted the land. Records reveal that a building on the site in 1687 was known by this name, and inside the main bar is a beautiful mosaic floor with the inscription 'Kings Arms Hotel'. The mosaic was laid more than three hundred years ago by some Italian masons working at the palace.

It still retains three bars, each with a different theme and its own atmosphere. The Wives Bar, for instance, has pictures of the six wives of Henry VIII looking at you from under the bar.

🍽 *11.00-11.00 Mon-Sat; 12.00-10.30 Sun.*
🍺 *Badger Black Adder, Dorset Best, IPA, King's Arms Bitter, Tanglefoot, Hall & Woodhouse seasonal ales. Cider: Blackthorn.*
🍴 *9.00-9.30 Mon-Sun.* Ⓥ
Open from 9.00 am for breakfast.
SYMBOLS: ❄ 🚹 🐕 ❎ 🍴
TEL: *020 8977 1729*

FOX ON THE RIVER
QUEENS ROAD, THAMES DITTON, SURREY

This large 1930s-style building has good views of Hampton Court Palace. Until 1996 it was called the Albany, after Lord Darnley who was given the title of Duke of Albany following his marriage to Mary Queen of Scots in 1565. When it was refurbished, in 1996, it was given a new identity.

One of its best features is the riverside garden. The pub provides a ferry service to the opposite bank at certain times of the year.

🍽 *12.00-11.00 Mon-Sat; 12.00-10.30 Sun.*
🍺 *Draught Bass, Fuller's London Pride. Cider: Blackthorn.*
🍴 *12.00-9.30 Mon-Sat; 12.00-9.00 Sun.* Ⓥ
SYMBOLS: 🅿 ❄ 🚹 🐕 ⛱ ❎ 🎣
TEL: *020 8339 1111*

YE OLDE SWAN

SUMMER ROAD, THAMES DITTON, SURREY

Parts of this listed building are said to date from the 13th century. One of its most famous customers was Henry VIII, who would have passed the inn on his way by boat from London to Hampton Court.

The pub has obviously been extended and seen many other changes in its long life. The interior is huge and clean, with exposed brickwork, old beams and atmospheric lighting, while a large open inglenook fireplace in the Tudor Room provides warmth in winter. A classic pub.

🏠 *11.00-11.00 Mon-Sat; 12.00-10.30 Sun.*

🍺 *Draught Bass, Courage Best, Greene King Abbot, IPA & Triumph, regular guest beer in summer. Cider: Scrumpy Jack, Strongbow.*

🍽 *12.00-2.30, 6.00-9.30 Mon-Fri; 12.00-9.30 Sat, Sun.* Ⓥ
Food served 12.00-9.30 every day in summer.

SYMBOLS: 🅿 ❄ 👫 🐕 🏛 🚬

TEL: *020 8398 1814*

Above Ye Olde Swan, Thames Ditton

THE BISHOP OUT OF RESIDENCE

BISHOPS HALL, THAMES STREET, KINGSTON-UPON-THAMES, SURREY

Built in 1979 on the site of an old leather tannery, this two-storey, brick, riverside pub has not yet been established long enough to gain a historical record – but its unusual name has. The intention was to call it the Kingston Ram, after the Young's brewery's trademark, but because there was already a Ram in the town this would undoubtedly have led to confusion. So the chairman of Young's asked the shareholders for some suggestions. The chosen title refers to the late-14th century residence of William Wykeham, the Bishop of Winchester and Lord Chancellor.

The sign depicts the Bishop out of Residence fishing on the Thames. An excellent stopping point in Kingston.

🖩 *11.00-11.00 Mon-Sat; 12.00-10.30 Sun.*
🍺 *Young's Bitter & Special, Young's seasonal beer. Cider: Strongbow.*
🍽 *11.00-4.00 Mon-Sat, 12.00-4.00 Sun, 5.00-8.00 Mon-Sun.* Ⓥ
SYMBOLS: 🎴 👫 🖼
TEL: *020 8546 4965*

THE WHITE HART

1 HIGH STREET, HAMPTON WICK, SURREY

An inn on this site was first recorded before 1658; the present building is in the mock-Tudor style with a combination of stone, brick, black wooden beams and leaded-light windows. The Tudor theme continues inside with oak panelling, large wooden doors with suitably large hinges that you expect to creak when opened, and old fireplaces, all blended together with tasteful decorations.

On a fine day you can sit outside on the patio and admire the colourful mural on the side wall of an adjoining building. It was painted by a local artist who specialises in exterior works of art and depicts an old

riverside wharf scene, with the chimney of the Fuller's brewery in the background.

This is one of the many Fuller's pubs that offers a traditional English menu at lunchtimes. But in the evenings magnificent spicy dishes from Thailand are on offer, all served in the informal atmosphere of a pub.

🕐 *11.00-11.00 Mon-Sat; 12.00-10.30 Sun.*

🍺 *Fuller's Chiswick Bitter, ESB & London Pride, Fuller's seasonal beer. Cider: Scrumpy Jack, Strongbow.*

🍴 *12.30-3.00 Mon-Sun, 6.00-9.45 Mon-Sat.* Ⓥ

SYMBOLS: 🅿 ❄ 👪 🐕 🍴 ♿ 🎪

TEL: *020 8977 1786*

THE BOATER'S INN
LOWER HAM ROAD, KINGSTON-UPON-THAMES, SURREY

If you fancy escaping the hustle and bustle of main town Kingston, take a gentle stroll along the towpath towards Teddington, where you will soon discover the Boater's Inn. The pub, sited as you might expect next to a rowing club, has been there just over ten years though the building itself is slightly older, having been a café before.

Slightly raised above the towpath, which is very handy should the river be in flood, the inn provides an excellent platform from which to view the river and the many cyclists who pass by the front door. Although it is a young inn, it is fast gaining a reputation for the quantity and quality of real ales it sells.

11.00-3.00, 5.30-11.00 Mon-Thurs; 11.00-11.00 Sat; 12.00-10.30 Sun.
Open all day during permitted hours from April to September.
5 changing guest beers. Cider: Blackthorn.
12.00-2.30, 7.00-9.30 Mon-Sun. ⓥ

SYMBOLS: ✳ 👫 🐕 🔁

TEL: *020 8541 4672*

THE TIDE END COTTAGE
8/10 FERRY ROAD, TEDDINGTON, MIDDLESEX

The name Teddington was at one time said to be derived from 'tide end town', which never seemed to find any credence with the learned scholars who lived here though the theory lives on in the name of this old inn. It nestles in a row of Victorian cottages opposite Teddington Lock, where the freshwater river meets the mighty tidal waters of the Thames. Originally, these dwellings would have housed boatmen and fishermen who earned their living from the river.

The open conservatory at the back of the pub contains a grapevine planted more than 25 years ago. It is said to be a cutting from the famous vine at nearby Hampton Court, planted in 1769 and itself a cutting from the Black Hamburgh vine at Valentines Park in Essex.

As you would expect, the small but cosy bars house river artefacts,

such as rowing memorabilia and stuffed fish. To maintain the association with fish, the pub serves what can only be described as a 'Moby Dick' portion of cod, dished up on a large oval platter.

While the sign outside denotes this as being a free house, this is not strictly true as the pub is now operated by one of the regional brewers, but this does not detract from its being a great hostelry.

🖼 *11.00-11.00 Mon-Sat; 12.00-10.30 Sun.*
🍺 *Draught Bass, Courage Best, Greene King Abbot & IPA, Marston's Pedigree. Cider: Strongbow.*
🍽 *12.00-2.30, 6.00-9.00 Mon-Sat; 12.00-5.00, 6.00-8.00 Sun.* Ⓥ
SYMBOLS: ❄ 🚻 🖼 🍽
TEL: *020 8977 7762*

THE ANGLERS
3 BROOM ROAD, TEDDINGTON, MIDDLESEX

At the end of the 18th century the area around Teddington would have consisted of farmland with the river providing a source of employment for the fishermen in the area. To cater for these and others working on the Thames, the Anglers Tavern was founded in 1795 and went on to become a grand hotel.

As with so many riverside hostelries it no longer provides accommodation, but is open all hours to serve a wide range of customers. It is very popular in fine weather because of the large terrace bordering the Thames. Regular barbecues are a feature.

🖼 *11.00-11.00 Mon-Sat; 12.00-10.30 Sun.*
🍺 *Marston's Pedigree, Morland Old Speckled Hen, Tetley Bitter, Young's Bitter. Cider: Blackthorn.*
🍽 *12.00-2.30, 6.00-9.00 Mon-Sat; 12.00-3.30 Sun.* Ⓥ
SYMBOLS: 🅿 ❄ 🚻 🖼 🍴 🏴 🍽
TEL: *020 8977 4178*

Above The Anglers, Teddington

BARMY ARMS

RIVERSIDE, TWICKENHAM, MIDDLESEX

This riverside pub started life in 1727 sedately called the Queen's Head. There are two theories of how it came by its current designation. The first and most popular with the locals is that a past landlord was considered by many to be absolutely barmy because of his eccentric and odd behaviour. The second and perhaps more feasible explanation refers to the froth on top of fermenting ale, called the barm. Being frothy or empty-headed would often be referred to as being barmy.

At one time the silly theme was exaggerated: the exterior sign was hung upside-down and the male/female designations on the toilet doors were the wrong way round. They are now in their correct places.

🔲 *11.00-11.00 Mon-Sat; 12.00-10.30 Sun.*

🔲 *Courage Best & Directors, regular guest beer. Cider: Strongbow.*

🔲 *12.00-2.30, 6.00-9.00 Mon-Sun.* Ⓥ

SYMBOLS: ❄️ 👭 🔲 🏠 🍴

TEL: *020 8892 0863*

THE WHITE SWAN

RIVERSIDE, TWICKENHAM, MIDDLESEX

There is nothing unique about the name of this popular riverside pub, but the same cannot be said of the pub itself. It can be found in a quiet street, so near, yet so far away from the main town centre.

There is some dispute about exactly when it opened as an inn, but it's thought to be between 1690 and 1722. A short flight of stairs takes you to the first floor bar, but don't expect any grand furnishings: this is a traditional pub in every sense of the word though the wooden floorboards, smoke-stained walls and ceilings and sparse furnishings are in their own way beautiful.

Two viewing areas are available to oversee the river: an outside balcony and the triclinium, a three-sided room with window seats.

🎫 *11.00-3.00, 5.30-11.00 Mon-Thur; 11.00-11.00 Fri, Sat; 12.00-10.30 Sun. Open all day during permitted hours from Easter to September.*

🍺 *Charles Wells Bombardier, Courage Best, Marston's Pedigree, Morland Old Speckled Hen. Cider: Scrumpy Jack, Strongbow.*

🍴 *12.00-2.30 Mon-Sun, 7.00-9.00 Mon-Thurs.* Ⓥ

SYMBOLS: ❄ 👬 🎫 🍺

TEL: *020 8892 2166*

Above The White Swan, Twickenham

RICHMOND
TO
FULHAM

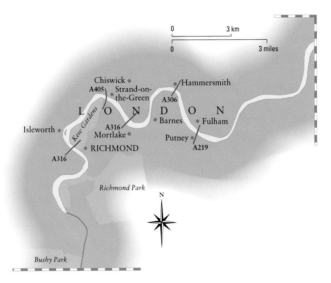

0   3 km

0   3 miles

Chiswick •
A405 • Strand-on-
the-Green
• Hammersmith

A306

L   O   N   D   O   N

Kew Gardens

A316
Mortlake •
• Barnes   • Fulham

Isleworth •

• RICHMOND
Putney •
A219

A316

Richmond Park

N

Bushy Park

The river from Twickenham flows past Richmond Hill, from
where one of the most commanding views of the Thames can
be seen. Wick House, on top of the hill, was built for the
famous painter Sir Joshua Reynolds.

Richmond-upon-Thames, on the Surrey side of the river, is well worth exploring. There are numerous buildings in the area with memorable histories; one of the town's many famous structures is the gateway and Old Palace yard of Richmond Palace. The palace itself was demolished in the 18th century but in the 15th and 16th centuries it was a favourite royal home, and Elizabeth I died there in 1603.

From Richmond the river passes Old Deer Park, where the British Architect Sir William Chambers designed and built the Kew Observatory for George III in 1769. Across the water lies the charming village of Isleworth: Vincent Van Gogh taught here at one stage and used the Thames as subject matter for his pupils.

The next section of the river gives the traveller the last chance to escape the built-up river banks, as it flows past the Syon Park estate landscaped by Capability Brown on one side and the famous Kew Botanical Gardens founded in 1759, on the other.

A complete contrast, though only a stone's throw from the wonders of Kew, are the tower blocks and old riverside warehouses of Brentford, once the county town of Middlesex. Here the Thames joined with the Grand Union Canal and opened up the waterway routes to many parts of the country in the late 18th century.

After Kew Bridge comes Strand-on-the-Green. This small hamlet has become one of the most fashionable places to live in West London. Before there was a river crossing, the local ferryman, who provided boat travel across the river for a fee, saw the potential in something more permanent, so in 1749 he built the very first bridge across the Thames in Kew. Strand-on-the-Green is a glorious village, with a striking riverside walkway and old fishermen's cottages covered with climbing clematis and wisteria. Beware if you visit at high tide as the footpath is prone to flooding. The Welsh poet Dylan Thomas, perhaps best known for *Under Milk Wood*, lived at Ship House Cottage while working in London as a journalist.

The river continues through the first of several double bends before coming to Mortlake. Each of its fine 18th-century riverside houses is

Right Bell & Crown, Strand-on-the-Green

distinguished by a different exterior colour. Chiswick Bridge marks the end of the annual Oxford and Cambridge Boat Race.

Barnes village lies in the horseshoe-shaped contour of the river. It has been home to a number of well-known thespians and other artists: Gustav Holst, composer of 'The Planets' orchestral suite, once lived at Barnes Terrace, which borders the river.

On the north bank lies Chiswick, a wonderful stretch of the river from Strand-on-the-Green through to Hammersmith. Houses in this part of West London are very much sought after and those by the river are at a premium. Chiswick House, an 18th-century miniature Palladian villa, has been described by David Piper as 'the most elegantly sophisticated public amenity of London' – in other words a marvellous house that is now open to everyone.

Some of the best parts of Hammersmith are on the riverside. Take a walk to find some excellent examples of bygone architecture such as the 18th-century Kelmscott House, named by William Morris after his country manor in Kelmscot. For some reason he added an extra t to the name of both his residences. There are also some fine waterside pubs where you can enjoy all the sights of the Thames, including the many rowers in this area.

Passing Hammersmith Bridge – the first London suspension bridge – built by Sir Joseph Bazalgette in 1883, the river flows past the well-known Harrod's Depository. It is no longer used by the store, but has been converted into residential apartments.

Fulham, on the north side of the river, was once well known for its market gardens serving the great city of London: now the only gardens you will find belong to the area's residents. It also has quite a sporting theme: Fulham Palace Football Ground is next to the river and the Queen's Tennis Club is nearby. On the other bank, after the Barns Elms Reservoir, comes Putney Embankment, location of many rowing clubs. It is virtually impossible to walk along this stretch without seeing the rowers practising. The start of the Oxford and Cambridge Boat Race is by the Star & Garter – once a famous pub, now, sadly, a theme bar.

THE ROSE OF YORK
PETERSHAM ROAD, RICHMOND, SURREY

This inn is sited in the shadow of the palatial Petersham Hotel. It was converted from the old stables during the last century and, though it presents an unassuming exterior, the inside will give you a pleasant surprise. Extensive oak panelling, bench seating, Georgian leaded-light windows and a host of other tasteful furnishings all blend to provide a comfortable setting.

▪ *11.00-11.00 Mon-Sat; 12.00-10.30 Sun.*
▪ *Samuel Smith Old Brewery Bitter. Cider: Samuel Smith Cider Reserve.*
▪ *12.00-2.30, 7.00-9.30 Mon-Fri; 12.00-9.30 Sat, Sun.* Ⓥ
SYMBOLS: 🅿 ✳ 🏠 🏠 ❄ 🍴 📷 ✏ 🏛
TEL: *020 8948 5867*

THE WATERMAN'S ARMS
12 WATER LANE, RICHMOND, SURREY

Possibly the oldest pub in Richmond, it started life around 1660 as the King's Head, but by 1669 the name had changed to the Waterman's Arms.

The lane in which it's situated also had various designations, such as Town Lane and Thames Lane, before becoming Water Lane, an obvious reference to its link with the river. At one stage it contained cottages housing the watermen and bargees who would have made their living from the river. There were other ways of earning money here: the house next to the pub was a brothel at a time when Water Lane was considered to be one of the most undesirable parts of town. In 1738 the then landlord of the Waterman's Arms, Thomas Collyer, together with his son and two other men were committed to the new gaol in Southwark by Justice Selvyn at Richmond for: 'Assaulting one Wells, a Fisherman of Chiswick, and wounding him in so dangerous a Manner with a Cutlass,

that his Life is despaired of: The Quarrel was occasioned by the Fishermans refusing to deliver his Net.'

The area must have been cleaned up, as an article in the Thames Valley News in 1956 described how the Swan Uppers, when they used to travel from Blackfriars Bridge to Henley, would stop at Richmond for lunch in the Waterman's Arms. Worth seeking out!

🕚 *11.00-3.00, 5.30-11.00 Mon-Fri; 11.00-11.00 Sat; 12.00-4.00, 7.00-10.30 Sun.*

🍺 *Young's Bitter & Special, Young's seasonal beer. Cider: Scrumpy Jack.*

🍽 *12.00-2.30 Mon-Sun.* Ⓥ

SYMBOLS: ❄ 🐎 ♨ 🍴

TEL: *020 8940 2893*

Above The Waterman's Arms, Richmond

THE WHITE CROSS
RIVERSIDE, RICHMOND, SURREY

To understand how this wonderful riverside hostelry obtained its title, we must look back to what originally stood on the site. The Convent of the Observant Friars, built by Henry VII in 1499, stood on a stretch from Friars Lane to Water Lane, its existence marked by the sign of a white cross. Catherine of Aragon asked to be buried there, but as the holy inmates had opposed Henry VIII's marriage to Anne Boleyn, the King would not allow her this privilege. The first record of there being a drinking house on the site was in 1780. It was thought to have been a watermen's tavern, but this was demolished to make way for the present Grade III listed building erected in 1835.

Due to the rising high-water tides, it is quite possible at certain times of the year to have your exit cut off, which would give you longer than you might have planned to explore the aged interior and wonder at how it came to have a very rare fireplace sited beneath one of the windows! Another unusual item, which sometimes goes unnoticed, is the Greek whitebeam tree in the front garden, which is reputed to be the only one in this country outside of Kew Gardens.

🕐 *11.00-11.00 Mon-Sat;*
12-10.30 Sun.
🍺 *Young's Bitter & Special, Young's seasonal beer. Cider: Scrumpy Jack.*
🍴 *12.00-4.00 Mon-Sun.* Ⓥ
SYMBOLS: ❄️ 🚹 🐕 🖼️
TEL: *020 8940 6844*

THE WHITE SWAN
26 OLD PALACE LANE, RICHMOND, SURREY

The story of the White Swan begins in 1760, some 17 years before the current building was erected. Sir Charles Asgill, City banker and former Lord Mayor of London, was in need of a country villa in which to relax as well as a venue for entertaining his influential friends. He commissioned the architect Sir Robert Taylor to build him a Palladian-style villa, which became known as Asgill House. A number of years later, a terrace of 12 small workmen's cottages, named Bath Buildings, was built in the lane beside the grand house. A small public house was also erected here which, due to its famous neighbour, was called the Asgill's Arms, and much of its custom came from the artisans who lived in the lane. In the 1851 census it was recorded that the Bath Buildings housed a number of tradesmen, including bricklayers, stonemasons and upholsterers and, more unusually, a yeast manufacturer and a straw bonnet maker. It is not known when the pub was renamed the White Swan.

By the 1950s the building was in a state of decline and disrepair but underwent major refurbishment by the brewers who owned it at the time to secure its future as a popular and enchanting riverside inn.

🔲 *11.00-3.00, 5.30-11.00 Mon-Fri; 11.00-11.00 Sat; 12.00-10.30 Sun.*
🔲 *Courage Best & Directors, Marston's Pedigree, Morland Old Speckled Hen. Cider: Strongbow.*
🔲 *12.00-2.30, 6.00-9.30 Mon-Sun.* Ⓥ
SYMBOLS: ❄ 👫 🔲 🍺
TEL: *020 8940 0959*

THE LONDON APPRENTICE
62 CHURCH STREET, ISLEWORTH, MIDDLESEX

The name of this famous inn on the banks of the Thames, where the Romans crossed in AD 54, may come from the ballad 'The honour of an apprentice of London' or it may refer to the young apprentices of the City livery companies, who would row up river on their rare days off. There has been an inn on this site for over five hundred years: the present three-storey building dates from the 18th century. From 1731, when it was first licensed, until 1739 it would stay open all night to serve the travellers arriving by road or by river. During its history many famous – and infamous – people sought refreshment at the inn: Henry VIII, Lady Jane Grey (Queen for nine days in 1553), Elizabeth I, Charles II and his mistress Nell Gwynne, and even the Puritan Oliver Cromwell. The highwayman Dick Turpin once arrived on horseback. Sir John Alcock and Sir Arthur Whitten-Brown, early innovators of flying machines, visited regularly during the First World War, before achieving their non-stop flight across the Atlantic in 1919. A plaque above the fireplace commemorates the occasion on 10 February 1848 when five bell-ringers, conducted by a Mr Nowell, completed a peal of 5,093 changes of Grandsire Caters in a record three hours, twenty minutes.

▪ *11.00-11.00 Mon-Sat; 12.00-10.30 Sun.*
▪ *Courage Best & Directors, Wadworth 6X. Cider: Strongbow.*
▪ *11.00-2.30, 6.00-9.30 Mon-Sat; 12.00-3.30 Sun.* ⓥ
SYMBOLS: 🅿 ❋ 👥 🐾 ⛴ 🐕 🎪
TEL: *020 8560 1915*

Rose & Crown

79 KEW GREEN, RICHMOND, SURREY

The sign of the rose and crown indicates loyalty to England and her monarch. It is thought that the original pub bearing this name was located at the foot of Kew Bridge on the other side of the main road leading to Richmond, and that it moved to its present site during the 18th century.

It started life in its new position in some old cottages, which were altered over the years to suit the layout of a busy hostelry, but in the 1930s the building was demolished to make way for the present mock-Tudor structure. The theme of the period extends inside with dark wood-panelled walls, red velvet seating and sedate furnishings, providing a quiet but atmospheric pub.

11.00-11.00 Mon-Sat; 12.00-10.30 Sun.

Courage Best & Directors, regular guest beer. Cider: Strongbow.

12.00-3.30, 7.00-10.30 Mon-Sun. Ⓥ

SYMBOLS:

TEL: *020 8940 2078*

BELL & CROWN
11-13 THAMES ROAD, STRAND-ON-THE-GREEN, LONDON

The Bell & Crown was licensed as an alehouse in 1751, two years after the very first bridge over the Thames was built here. It received much of its custom from travellers using the new crossing. Such a name normally signifies the ringing of bells on royal occasions, but this inn's new sign, standing high above the riverbank, tells another story – that of smuggling. The area was once rife with fishermen who, to avoid paying duty on imported goods, would collect the bounty from the many ships in the Port of London and bring them up river. Sometimes the goods were stored in pub cellars before being whisked away to their final destination.

The old building was demolished in 1907 to make way for the present structure, complete with a conservatory and patio overlooking this pleasant part of the river.

11.00-11.00 Mon-Sat; 12.00-10.30 Sun.
Fuller's Chiswick Bitter, ESB & London Pride, Fuller's seasonal beer.
Cider: Strongbow.
12.30-10.00 Mon-Sun. Ⓥ
SYMBOLS: ❋ 👫 🐕 🏠 ✖
TEL: *020 8994 4164*

THE CITY BARGE
27 STRAND-ON-THE-GREEN, LONDON

An inn so truly riverside that the watertight door to the lower bar has to be bolted and secured when high tides are forecast. This old hostelry started life as the Navigators Arms in 1484, an obvious reference to the river. Elizabeth I at sometime during her long reign between 1558 and 1603, granted the inn a royal charter of rights for a period of five hundred years. There is a rare example of an open-faced parliamentary clock inside the bar. They were made in the 18th century when the William Pitt the Younger, England's youngest-ever prime minister, introduced 'assessed taxes', which included a levy on windows and clock faces with hinged glass.

Towards the end of the 18th century, the pub changed to its present name after the *Maria Wood*, the Lord Mayor of London's barge, which

was moored in this reach of the river. During a heavy bombing raid in the Second World War, the pub suffered extensive damage. When it was restored, some salvaged parts of the original structure were incorporated.

🔟 *11.00-11.00 Mon-Sat; 12.00-10.30 Sun.*
🍺 *Courage Best & Directors, Theakston's XB & Old Peculiar. Cider: Strongbow.*
🍴 *11.30-10.00 Mon-Sun; 12.00-10.00 Sun.* Ⓥ
SYMBOLS: 🅿 ❄ 🚻 🔟 🍴
TEL: *020 8994 2148*

Above The City Barge, Strand-on-the-Green

THE SHIP
10 THAMES BANK,
MORTLAKE, LONDON

This inn, which is thought to be the oldest in Mortlake, has changed its name many times in its 400-year history. It started as the Hart's Horn, became the Hartshorns, then changed to the Blue Anchor, which was later shortened to the Anchor. When it was rebuilt in the 19th century it changed yet again to the Ship.

Its neighbour, the Mortlake Brewery, has been in existence since 1487 so a supply of local beer has never been a problem – until it switched to lager production only. Refurbished in 1998, the pub has the standard interior layout of modern furnishings favoured by its operator.

Every year the embankment here becomes packed with spectators who have gathered to witness the Oxford and Cambridge Boat Race teams crossing the finishing line just before Chiswick Bridge.

11.00-11.00 Mon-Sat; 12.00-10.30 Sun.
Courage Best & Directors, Theakston's XB. Cider: Strongbow.
11.00-10.00 Mon-Sat; 12.00-10.00 Sun. Ⓥ
SYMBOLS: P ✳ ⛹ 🐕
TEL: *020 8876 1439*

YE WHITE HART
THE TERRACE, RIVERSIDE, BARNES, LONDON

The earliest reference to an inn on this site goes back to 1676, when it was known as the King's Arms. It kept this name until the mid-18th century, when the Trevvy family of Putney, who held the pub at the time, changed it to the White Hart. The established Wandsworth brewers Young & Bainbridge purchased the premises, which the Young's company (the partnership with Bainbridge was dissolved in 1884) still owns. It hosted the meetings of the Rose of Denmark Lodge of the Freemasons for a period of 15 years at the end of the 19th century.

The pub was rebuilt in 1899 in the grand Victorian style, consisting of four storeys, a circular staircase and the provision of three open balconies at the rear. The large open-plan interior, with high ceilings, ornate columns and marble fireplaces, at one time housed four bars: public, saloon, lounge and private snug. The prints and paintings of Ye White Hart all around the walls give a pictorial story of its past.

With such a commanding view of the river from the back terraces, the pub is, as you would expect, packed to the gunnels on the day of the Oxford and Cambridge Boat Race, but it's popular and busy at all other times of the year. In addition to the excellent Young's ales available, its selection of wines has won it the prestigious Wine Pub of the Year award a number of times.

Above Ye White Hart, Barnes

175

▦ *11.00-3.00, 5.30-11.00 Mon-Thurs; 11.00-11.00 Fri, Sat;*
12.00-10.30 Sun.
▦ *Young's Bitter & Special, Young's seasonal beer. Cider: Blackthorn.*
▦ *12.00-2.30 Mon-Sun.* Ⓥ
SYMBOLS: ▦ ▦ ▦
TEL: *020 8876 5177*

THE BULL'S HEAD
373 LONSDALE ROAD, BARNES, LONDON

Once upon a time, before the fashionable urban village of Barnes sprang up, this area around the river would have consisted of farmland. The pub is built on the site of a farmhouse and started life as the King's Head. It was first mentioned in records dated 1672. Nearly 80 years later the name was changed to the Bull's Head. In 1847 the building was refurbished by the owner, John Waring, whose family had acquired a number of properties around Barnes Terrace. The busy wharf that used to be adjacent would have provided much of its custom, but when this closed the pub's business suffered, forcing it into a period of decline.

However, in November 1959 Albert Tolley began staging jazz concerts at the Bull's Head, and these proved to be its salvation. It is now an international venue, as can be seen from the list in the bar of the famous musicians who have performed for the people who flock here to hear great sounds.

The interior is open plan, with an island bar and a purpose-built auditorium for the music sessions.

▦ *11.00-11.00 Mon-Sat; 12-10.30 Sun.*
▦ *Young's Bitter & Special, Young's seasonal beer. Cider: Blackthorn.*
▦ *12.00-2.30, 6.00-11.00 Mon-Sun.* Ⓥ
SYMBOLS: ▦ ▦ ▦ ▦ ▦
TEL: *020 8876 5241*

THE MAWSON ARMS/THE FOX & HOUNDS
110 CHISWICK LANE SOUTH, CHISWICK, LONDON

There are too many stories that explain how this pub came to have two names, so perhaps the easiest thing to do is to make up a story of your own. What is certain is that Thomas Mawson arrived in Chiswick some time in the 1680s and, within 20 years, had laid the foundations of a great brewing empire that would, in time, be taken over by three partners – Fuller, Smith and Turner.

The three-storey building housing the pub, known as Mawsons Row, was obviously built by either Thomas Mawson or his son with the same name, who inherited the business on his father's death in 1714. The Mawson Arms was once a private house where Alexander Pope lived with his parents from 1716 to 1719. While he was here, Pope translated the greater part of Homer's epic work the *Iliad*.

The pub is now very much the official brewery tap, its best recommendation being the number of Fuller's brewery staff who drink here. It is also the starting point for regular tours

of the brewery, so if you would like to see how one of London's greatest brewers makes beer, then this is the place to head for.

🔳 *11.00-9.00 Mon-Fri; 12.00-4.00 Sun; closed Sat.*
🍺 *Fuller's Chiswick Bitter, ESB & London Pride, Fuller's seasonal beer. Cider: Scrumpy Jack.*
🍴 *12.00-8.30 Mon-Fri; 12.00-3.30 Sun.* ⓥ
SYMBOLS: 🔲
TEL: *020 8994 2936*

THE OLD SHIP
25 UPPER MALL, HAMMERSMITH, LONDON

There used to be a large landing stage outside this 19th-century riverside hostelry – the remains of the wooden posts that supported it can still be seen at low tide. In 1914, a proposal was put forward to flatten the Old Ship to make way for a factory development on the banks of the Thames. However, the Royal Humane Society used the landing stage for storing life-saving equipment so the plans were abandoned and the pub survived.

The theme of ships and boats extends through the modern interior of the pub, with a variety of nautical artefacts embellishing the walls and ceilings. For those of you who like to sample something different, why not try one of the vodkas that are flavoured with such diverse ingredients as garlic or Mars Bar?

🔳 *11.00-11.00 Mon-Sat; 12.00-10.30 Sun.*
🍺 *Fuller's London Pride, Morland Old Speckled Hen, Wadworth 6X. Cider: Strongbow.*
🍴 *11-10.30 Mon-Sat; 12.00-10.00 Sun.* ⓥ
Breakfast served from 10.00 (9.00 Sat, Sun).
SYMBOLS: ❄ 🚹 🔲
TEL: *020 8748 2593*

THE DOVE
UPPER MALL, HAMMERSMITH, LONDON

Apart from a few 20th-century mod-cons, you get the impression that not much has changed in this splendid 17th-century waterside inn, which everyone should visit at least once in their lifetime. Over the years, many celebrated people have paid a call to this small inn tucked away down a narrow alleyway. Charles II and Nell Gwynne would arrive incognito, this being made easier by its location. In one of the upstairs rooms, the Scottish poet, James Thomson, penned the words of 'Rule Britannia', which was set to music by Thomas Arne. A score sheet of the song hangs on the wall of the bar, but it has never been authenticated as the original.

In 1860, the Dove became the Doves, when the artist who was repainting the sign was overcome with enthusiasm and put in two birds instead of the intended one. It reverted to the singular in 1948.

According to *The Guinness Book of Records*, the pub has the smallest public bar in England. It's 1.3m x 2.4m, or 3.12 square metres, and there is an unofficial record of the number of people that can be squeezed into a room of this size – it's 35.

There is an excellent viewing area over the river, complete with a thriving grape-vine.

🔲 *11.00-11.00 Mon-Sat; 12.00-10.30 Sun.*
🍺 *Fuller's ESB & London Pride, Fuller's seasonal beer. Cider: Strongbow*
🍴 *12.00-3.00, 6.30-9.30 Mon-Sat; 12.00-4.00, 6.30-9.30 Sun.* Ⓥ
SYMBOLS: ❄ 🔲 🏠
TEL: *020 8748 5405*

Opposite The Dove, Hammersmith

BLUE ANCHOR

13 LOWER MALL, HAMMERSMITH, LONDON

The colour blue represents hope, which accounts for its inclusion in the name of this inn overlooking the suspension bridge at Hammersmith. First licensed in the reign of George I, this pub has watched over the Thames for nearly three hundred years, seeing the twice-daily tides coming in and going out and bringing a variety of surprises to the shores.

Gustav Holst, the composer who lived locally, perhaps best remembered for the orchestral suite 'The Planets' wrote his 'Hammersmith Suite' in this pub.

Bedecking the interior of this small pub is a selection of ornaments from the Second World War, as well as the customary skiffs and oars that you'd expect, given the number of rowing clubs in the area.

An abundance of outside tables provides the opportunity to soak up the atmosphere of one of the most popular parts of the Thames path.

🕐 *11.00-11.00 Mon-Sat; 12.00-10.30 Sun.*
🛢 *Courage Best & Directors, regular guest beer. Cider: Strongbow.*
🍴 *11.00-10.00 Mon-Sat; 12.00-10.00 Sun.* Ⓥ
SYMBOLS: ❄ 👥 🕐 🍽
TEL: *020 8748 5774*

THE CRABTREE TAVERN
RAINVILLE ROAD, FULHAM, LONDON

This attractive riverside pub is hidden away in the maze of Edwardian terraced houses in this popular part of Fulham. It was built in 1898 to serve the workers employed on the wharves that used to line the river, as well as the inhabitants of the vast Crabtree Estate being built on the land that used to form part of the local market gardens. Very much a community pub, the loyalty of its customers was put to the test during the Second World War when one night all its windows were blown out by a bomb falling close by. The next morning it was business as usual but as there was no beer available – the faithful customers chose to drink lemonade instead!

Following a major redevelopment in the 1980s the pub was renamed the Jolly Gardeners. But once again the locals rallied together, incensed by this unthinkable act of treachery, and only a couple of months later the name was changed back and harmony was restored.

🍴 *11.00-11.00 Mon-Sat; 12.00-10.30 Sun.*
🍺 *Courage Best & Directors, Theakston's Best, occasional guest beer.*
Cider: Strongbow.
🍽 *11.00 (12.00 Sun)-10.00 Mon-Sun.* Ⓥ
SYMBOLS: ❄ 👫 🍴 🍽
TEL: *020 7385 3929*

DUKE'S HEAD
8 LOWER RICHMOND ROAD, PUTNEY, LONDON

In 1832 when Wandsworth brewer Young & Bainbridge first took on the lease, the Duke's Head not only functioned as a public house but also did a roaring trade in serving teas to those enjoying a gentle stroll by the riverside. Someone there must have had some foresight, or perhaps some inside knowledge, as in 1845 the Oxford and Cambridge

Boat Race was moved from its Henley course to the tidal waters of the Thames at Putney. The university stone, overlooked by the pub, marks the starting point of what is one of London's greatest sporting spectacles.

In 1864 the pub was rebuilt, providing the three-storey structure with commanding views over the river that stands today. For reasons not recorded the structure was altered in 1894, which may have prompted what was now Young & Co. to buy the freehold of the property in 1899.

Internally the pub has retained its Victorian splendour, with high ceilings, decorative lamps, ornate woodwork, splendid etched glass panels and exquisite furnishings. The large windows in the lounge bar provide a marvellous area to watch the activities on the river and the sun setting in the west.

11.00-11.00 Mon-Sat; 12-10.30 Sun.
Young's Bitter & Special, Young's seasonal beer. Cider: Scrumpy Jack.
12.00-2.30, 6.00-10.00 Mon-Sat; 12.00-3.00 Sun. Ⓥ
SYMBOLS: ❋ ⛎ ⛿
TEL: *020 8788 2552*

Above Duke's Head, Putney

THE EIGHT BELLS
89 FULHAM ROAD, FULHAM, LONDON

This grand three-storey building, sometimes hidden from view when the large tree in front is in full leaf, was at one time a thriving roadside inn on the main Hammersmith to Putney road. The original wooden toll bridge was built in 1729 and it lasted well for over two hundred and fifty years until, in 1884, the present crossing of Putney Bridge was built by Sir Joseph Bazalgette. Of course, until the new bridge was ready the old one could not be demolished, so to accommodate this the new crossing had to be installed slightly up river. Because the route of the high street had to change, owners of the premises were awarded what was then the large sum of £1,000 each, in compensation for their inconvenience and loss of trade.

The pub started life in around 1629 when it was originally known as the Bell Alehouse, but became known as the Eight Bells when an additional two bells were added to the local All Saints Church in 1729. The original three bars are now amalgamated into one drinking area, but the exterior antique frosted glass from Germany still protects the anonymity of the customers inside. This traditional drinking pub serves a cross section of customers in an unpretentious setting.

🕐 *11.00-11.00 Mon-Sat; 12.00-10.30 Sun.*
🍺 *Courage Best & Directors. Cider: Strongbow.*
🍽 *11.00-3.00 Mon-Sun, 5.00-8.00 Mon-Sun (summer only).* Ⓥ
SYMBOLS: ❄
TEL: *020 7736 6307*

Above The Eight Bells, Fulham

187

WANDSWORTH
TO
TOWER
BRIDGE

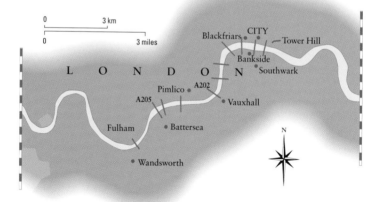

Wandsworth, which as well as being on the Thames is crossed
by the River Wandle, was a contender in the 18th century for
the most industrialised area in London.

One of the best-known buildings in the area is the Young's Ram Brewery, where beer has been brewed since 1581. If you are lucky, you may see one of the Young's horse-drawn drays.

From Wandsworth the river starts to become a working waterway. Until it reaches Battersea, the embankment comprises industrial units, factories, warehouses and wharves where goods are received and held before being taken by boat to other parts of the country.

Coming into Battersea, the area suddenly changes, reverting to a residential location. The church of St Mary, overlooking the river, is where Turner painted his Thames sunsets. Battersea's other claims to fame are its Dogs' Home (which also takes cats), the park which opened in 1853, and that blot on the landscape Battersea Power Station. It closed during the 1970s and, despite plans at one time to turn it into a theme park, the future of this listed building remains undecided.

From the dust of an old coal depot, rose Chelsea Harbour, an exclusive development of apartments, shops, a hotel and a marina. On top of the 20-storey apartment block is a coloured ball which rises and falls to show the position of the river-tide. Many of the walls of Cheyne Walk, at one time a riverside village, carry English Heritage blue plaques marking the homes of distinguished people, including Lloyd George, Hilaire Belloc and Isambard Kingdom Brunel. Chelsea Embankment contains many grand town houses, as well as the Chelsea Royal Hospital where the unmistakably uniformed Chelsea Pensioners live. Once a year their back garden becomes the venue for the Chelsea Flower Show.

Next we come to Pimlico on the north bank, a residential area popular with MPs because of its close proximity to the Houses of Parliament. Dolphin Square was constructed in 1937 and its 1,250 dwellings made it the largest block of flats in Europe at the time. Millbank, named after the mediaeval water mill that used to be on the banks of the Thames, was the site of a prison until its closure in 1890 and demolition two years later. One of the new buildings built in its place was the Tate Gallery, which opened in 1897 to house the collection of modern British paintings and other artefacts belonging to the sugar tycoon Henry Tate.

On the opposite bank is the Albert Embankment, built by Bazalgette in the mid-19th century. It runs from Vauxhall Bridge to Lambeth Bridge and is now the location of a number of office blocks including Vauxhall Cross, the offices of MI6.

Next is Westminster, one of the best-known parts of London and the nerve centre of British government. There is much to see here including Big Ben, the Houses of Parliament and Westminster Abbey, all with their own unique pasts and stories to tell.

The Thames now becomes a main feature of the capital and its route to Tower Bridge includes attractions on both embankments. There are regular boat trips from Westminster Pier to Greenwich. The excursion starts opposite County Hall, former home of the now defunct Greater London Council, and goes past Victoria Embankment which separates the river from many historic buildings such as Old Scotland Yard. Opposite are the concert halls of the South Bank Arts Centre, a memorial to the architects who considered concrete beautiful!

Passing Waterloo Bridge, the river takes a right turn and the beautiful St Paul's Cathedral soon comes into view. On the south bank the once plentiful warehouses have been replaced by new buildings including the London Television Centre. The Temple on the north bank derives its name from the Order of the Knights Templar, who resided in the area between the 12th and 14th centuries. Now famous for its Law Courts, the area requires exploring on foot as not much of it can be seen from the river.

From Blackfriars Bridge to London Bridge on the north side of the river is the City area of London – the Square Mile – which houses many financial and commercial institutions. Here you will find the Bank of England, the Guildhall, the Stock Exchange and the modern Lloyd's Building renowned for its insurance market. The south bank between the bridges is a mixed bag of edifices: the old Bankside Power Station, which was designed by Sir Giles Gilbert Scott, is being renovated and will become an extension to the Tate Gallery; next door is the new Globe Theatre, modelled on the second building of that name, which was demolished in 1644, and built using traditional materials. Other points of interest in this area are the Clink Prison Museum, a replica of the *Golden Hind*, the remains of Winchester Palace, Borough Market and Southwark Cathedral.

On the City side, the river runs past the Monument (built to mark the spot where the Great Fire of London started in 1666) and the old Billingsgate Fish Market, which was closed in 1982 and the trading moved to the Isle of Dogs. Next comes one of the most famous landmarks in the city – the Tower of London. The Tower has been used for many purposes in its centuries-old history, but perhaps is most notorious for its part in the imprisonment and execution of many famous people. Today the Tower is best known as the home of the Crown Jewels, overseen by Yeoman Warders, better known as Beefeaters and instantly recognisable by their red and black costumes. Black ravens live at the Tower and legend says that if they leave, the Kingdom will fall.

Crossing over London Bridge to the south side will reveal Hays Galleria – a modernisation of Hay's Wharf built by Cubitt in 1856. It consists of restaurants, shops and bars to cater for its many visitors. From the terrace you can see HMS *Belfast*, a ship that saw action in the Second World War and now a floating museum.

The final crossing, and certainly the grandest, is Tower Bridge, designed by Sir Horace Jones and Sir John Wolfe Barry in 1894. The two drawbridges, which weigh over 1,000 tons each, were originally powered by steam engines but it went all electric in 1975. In 1951, the quick-thinking driver of a bus caught on the bridge while the bascules were being raised increased his speed and jumped the gap with no damage done to his passengers or vehicle!

Above Signpost at Founder's Arms, Southwark

THE CAT'S BACK
86-88 POINT PLEASANT, WANDSWORTH, LONDON

As Wandsworth is home to Young's, one of the country's oldest brewers, it is understandable that there is a glut of their pubs in the area. Therefore when this free house opened in 1994, it was a brave move by the owner to provide an alternative.

Point Pleasant has not always lived up to its name: at one time it was an open sewer for Putney (or Putterhythe as it was known then). It is claimed that during a visit to the area Elizabeth I was so disgusted at what she saw that her sarcasm got the better of her when she said 'what a pleasant point'. After a spot of transposition, the name of the road was here to stay.

The building was first constructed in 1865 to serve the lightermen working on the river, transferring goods on their lighters from the ships to the wharves. During the course of its life, it has had an assortment of names and was owned by a number of brewers, none of whom were

Above The Cat's Back, Wandsworth

192

willing to spend any money on the premises. It finally fell into disrepair during the 1960s.

When it was brought back to life by the present owner, it started as the pub with no name – not called that, it simply didn't have a title. After some 18 anonymous months, the problem was solved by a course of events. The tale involves the landlord, his girlfriend, a missing cat called Chester and a three-week holiday, the barman and an 'A' board which quite simply said 'the Cat's back'.

All in all, a zany pub with a vast collection of strange artefacts that will make you wonder if you have walked into a pub or a secondhand shop.

🕐 *12.00-3.00 Mon-Sun, 5.30-11.00 Mon-Fri, 7.00-11.00 Sat, 7.00-10.30 Sun.*

🛢 *Draught Bass, O'Hanlons Blakeley's Best, O'Hanlons Myrica Ale (summer only). Cider: Strongbow, Hughs Organic Scrumpy (summer only).*

🍴 *12.00-3.00 Mon-Sun.* Ⓥ

SYMBOLS: 🚹 🕐 🍴

TEL: *020 8877 0818*

THE SHIP
41 JEWS ROW, WANDSWORTH, LONDON

Sited at the bottom of Jews Row, this old riverside pub is surrounded not by cobbled streets with old houses but by industrial units, not forgetting the ready-mixed concrete plant next door. In a funny way, this is not detrimental to the setting, but helps to paint a true picture of this area by the river.

The brightly coloured early 19th-century building stands in an area called

Bridge Field. Although Wandsworth Bridge did not open until 1873, a crossing for here may have been planned much earlier.

At one time the pub was surrounded by cottages, which one by one have been demolished to make more space available to the pub. A large patio by the river gives the opportunity to witness the busy comings and goings on the waterway. Tied up alongside the pub is the Thames sailing barge *Convoy*, built in 1900, which belongs to the present tenant.

The pub has two distinct bars and a conservatory was added in 1987. The informal modern saloon has wooden floors and fresh flowers on the tables. However, the public bar is like a trip back in time: it's a perfect example of how a 1930s bar would have looked. Old tables and chairs, an upright piano, bar stools and wooden hand pumps are all hidden from outside by antique frosted glass windows. There is even an old working range where sausages are cooked in winter. The pork and lamb used in the pub comes from the tenant's farm, which has recently been certified as totally organic.

🕔 *11.00-11.00 Mon-Sat; 12.00-10.30 Sun.*

🍺 *Young's Bitter & Special, Young's seasonal beer. Cider: Strongbow.*

🍴 *12.00-3.00 Mon-Fri, 12.00-4.00 Sat, Sun; 7.00-10.30 Mon-Sun. All day on Sat and Sun in summer.* Ⓥ

SYMBOLS: ❄ 👫 🔒 🍺

TEL: *020 8870 9667*

THE FERRET & FIRKIN IN THE BALLOON UP THE CREEK

114 LOTS ROAD, FULHAM, LONDON

Once holding the title of having the longest pub name in England, this was one of the original Firkin pubs opened by entrepreneur David Bruce in 1983. The style was very much 'spit & sawdust' with bare floorboards, sparse furnishings, cheap food and beer supplied by an on-site micro-brewery, which in this case was located in the cellar. Sadly this is now not used, and it's unlikely that the smell of boiling wort and hops will ever be experienced again in the Ferret and Firkin.

The pub was originally called the Balloon. It had a special licence to serve beer from 3.00 in the morning to the workers employed in the coal yards where the luxurious Chelsea Harbour now stands. A by-product of the manufacture of coke was low-gravity gas which was used for ballooning. Later it became known as the Balloon Up the Creek, which seemed a fitting epitaph as it ended up being derelict before it was firkinised. Still an excellent pub!

🕰 *12.00-11.00 Mon-Sat; 12.00-10.30 Sun.*
🍺 *Firkin Best, Dogbolter & Ferret Ale. Cider: Scrumpy Jack.*
🍴 *12.00-8.00 Mon-Sun.* Ⓥ
SYMBOLS: 🚹 📷 💺 🍴
TEL: *020 7352 6645*

THE RIVERSIDE
2 LOMBARD ROAD, BATTERSEA, LONDON

A modern-day pub on the ground floor of a residential apartment block by the river at Battersea. The large windows of the single-storey interior overlook the riverside terrace with the grandiose Chelsea Harbour in the background. It is a perfect place to sit enjoying a drink, watching the expensive yachts going in and out of the harbour, and thinking if only...

🕰 *12.00-11.00 Mon-Sat; 12.00-10.30 Sun.*
🍺 *Wadworth 6X*
🍴 *12.00-3.00, 6.30-10.00 Mon-Sun.* Ⓥ
All day in summer.
SYMBOLS: ❄ 🚹 📷 🍴
TEL: *020 7978 4167*

THE KING'S HEAD & EIGHT BELLS
50 CHEYNE WALK, CHELSEA, LONDON

When the Thames ran closer to the pub than it does now, it had the advantage of its own landing stage – called the Feather Stairs. Here royals travelling by river could moor their boats while they sought refreshment in the King's Head: the servants, though, would have had to use the Eight Bells. The two pubs were merged during the latter part of the 16th century, though both names were retained. Oliver Cromwell is said to have been a regular caller when he was Lord Protector.

Over the next three hundred years or so, the pub developed a relationship with the writers and artists living in this particularly pleasant part of Chelsea. Thomas Carlyle, the Scottish essayist and social historian, lived on Cheyne Row, built on what was originally a courtyard at the back of the pub. Then there was Turner, Dante Gabriel Rossetti, George Eliot, and the artist James Whistler – a regular in the pub who summed up his career with the words, 'it's just a matter of how you hold your pencil!'

The attractive building that stands before you today was erected some time in the 19th century and was one of thirteen pubs in Cheyne Walk, though it's now the only one remaining.

🕚 *11.00-11.00 Mon-Sat; 12.00-10.30 Sun.*
🍺 *Adnams Best, Flowers Original, Morland Old Speckled Hen, Wadworth 6X, occasional guest beer. Cider: Strongbow.*
🍴 *12.00-10.00 Mon-Sat; 12.30-4.00, 7.00-10.00 Sun.* Ⓥ
SYMBOLS: 👥 🔥 🍴
TEL: *020 7352 1820*

THE PRINCE ALBERT

85 ALBERT BRIDGE ROAD, BATTERSEA,
LONDON

This three-storey Victorian corner building opposite the western entrance to Battersea Park stands on a road leading to the Albert Bridge, a grand suspension crossing over the Thames built in 1873 and is a shrine to Albert, husband of Queen Victoria, who was made Prince Consort in 1857.

As with many pubs of that era the Prince Albert started life as a hotel, but converted to a drinking establishment when it was realised that there was more money in beer than beds. Now run by a large company, it is very contrived, but nevertheless has a nice atmosphere in which to enjoy a pleasant part of London.

As you would expect the large open interior pays tribute to the Prince Consort with paintings, prints and other memorabilia relating to him adorning the walls.

11.00-11.00 Mon-Sat; 12.00-10.30 Sun.
Courage Best, Theakston's Best, regular guest beer in summer. Cider: Strongbow.
11.00-9.30 Mon-Sat; 12.00-9.30 Sun. Ⓥ
SYMBOLS:
TEL: *020 7228 0923*

MORPETH ARMS

58 MILLBANK, PIMLICO, LONDON

The magnificent four-storey Grade II listed building housing the Morpeth Arms was built in 1845 by Paul Dangerfield, a specialist in this particular field of construction. The pub was named after Viscount Morpeth, the chief commissioner who redeveloped the area. Amongst its neighbours are the offices of two of the country's intelligence organisations – MI5 and MI6, so be careful what you say to whom when in the bar. There still exists a maze of tunnels beneath the pub, which it is said are visited by a long-deceased inmate of the now-demolished Millbank prison. He became lost in the labyrinth in the course of an escape attempt, never to be seen again.

The building was completely refurbished when it was taken over by the Young's brewery in 1984, but its original features and links with the past were carefully preserved.

🅼 *11.00-11.00 Mon-Sat; 12.00-10.30 Sun.*
🍺 *Young's Bitter & Special, Young's seasonal beer. Cider: Blackthorn.*
🍴 *11.30 (12.00 Sun)-8.00 Mon-Sun.* Ⓥ
SYMBOLS: ❄ 🚻 🐾 🅷
TEL: *020 7834 6442*

OLD FATHER THAMES
12 ALBERT EMBANKMENT, VAUXHALL, LONDON

With its name taken from a phrase first used by the poet Alexander Pope, in 1704, the Old Father Thames pub overlooks the river with the Houses of Parliament in the background from its position on the Albert Embankment. Built nearly forty years ago as part of Queensborough House, as a pub, it replaced the Red Cow which had stood on the site for many years.

An exterior concrete fascia paints a false picture of the interior, which is all wooden floors, high-backed settles, exposed brickwork and brewing memorabilia. The basement houses an atmospheric replica of a Victorian bar. The flagstone floors, low, intimate lighting and secluded seating arrangements make this the perfect place to escape from the busy London streets above.

▥ *11.00-11.00 Mon-Fri; closed Sat, Sun.*
▧ *Abroad Cooper, Boddingtons Bitter, Wadworth 6X, two occasional guest beers. Cider: Strongbow.*
▥ *12.00-8.00 Mon-Fri.* Ⓥ
SYMBOLS: ✳ ♟ ▥ ▨
TEL: *020 7735 7004*

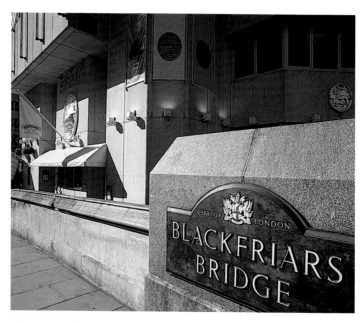

DOGGETT'S

1 BLACKFRIARS BRIDGE, SOUTHWARK, LONDON

This uniquely named four-storey pub, which stands at the southern end of Blackfriars bridge, rises above the crossing and oversees all the passing road and river traffic. It was erected in 1976 in a style that was very much in vogue at the time.

It owes its name to an 18th-century Irish comedian and actor, Thomas Doggett, who was responsible for the oldest continuous sporting event in the country – the annual sculling race for the prize of Doggett's Coat & Badge. As you would expect, there are several versions of how this race was started but the following tale seems to have most credence. One night Doggett found himself needing to get from London Bridge to Chelsea as quickly as possible. The most direct route was by river, but because the tide was flowing out to sea he had a lot of refusals, before he found a waterman willing to take him the five miles upstream. When

Above Doggett's, Southwark

they eventually reached Chelsea, the young man informed him that he had just finished his apprenticeship and had been rewarded with his freedom from the Company of Watermen and Lightermen. Doggett was so impressed that he tipped the rower generously and was struck with the idea of organising a race for six young watermen just out of their time. The first race took place on 1 August 1715 over the same course that he had taken, and the prize was an orange coat in honour of the then king, George I, with a silver badge inscribed with the White Horse of Hanover to denote liberty. Doggett died in 1721 but made provision in his will for a trust to be set up to ensure the race continued. It still happens, every July or August depending on the tides.

▥ *11.00-11.00 Mon-Fri; closed Sat, Sun.*
▣ *Fuller's London Pride, Marston's Pedigree, Morland Old Speckled Hen, Tetley Bitter, Wadworth 6X, regular guest beers. Cider: Blackthorn.*
⬓ *12.00-3.00.* Ⓥ
SYMBOLS: ✳ 👬 🍴 🍺
TEL: *020 7633 9081*

THE BLACKFRIAR
174 QUEEN VICTORIA STREET, BLACKFRIARS, LONDON

During the reign of Edward I, a Dominican priory was established in 1278 on what is now the site of the Blackfriar, a name taken from the colour of the monks' habits. The friars were considered to be highly intellectual, but they liked a drop of the hard stuff as well. After a long and colourful history, the monastery was dissolved in 1538, when the building was valued at £104 15s 15d.

The current building was erected in 1875 and was at the time surrounded by other structures linked by small dark alleyways. Over the years the pub's neighbours have slowly disappeared, leaving it to stand alone, with the strange wedge-shaped building looking as though it could topple over at any moment. The pub itself was facing demolition

in the 1960s, a period when the country's heritage was taking second place to virtually everything else. Fortunately the pub was saved by a band of people, including the poet Sir John Betjeman, who appreciated the finer things in life. A protection order now saves it from any future onslaught by bulldozers.

It is not only the exterior that is unique. The interior presents a sight unlikely to be equalled anywhere else. During a refurbishment at the beginning of the 20th century, the sculptor Henry Poole came up with a design so stunning that its usual label of 'art nouveau' fails to do it justice. The theme of friars continues throughout and marble is heavily featured. It doesn't need decorating, but the colour has probably changed considerably over the years, now with a smoke-stained finish. Domed ceilings, ornate mosaics and bronze sculptures depicting the happy monks and open gas lamps all provide a stunning surrounding.

It can get very busy at lunchtimes and in the early evenings.

11.30-11.00 Mon-Fri; 12.00-5.00 Sat; closed Sun.
Adnams Best, Brakspear Bitter, Marston's Pedigree, Tetley Bitter.
Cider: Blackthorn.
12.00-2.30 Mon-Sat; 5.30-9.00 Mon-Fri. Ⓥ
SYMBOLS: ❉
TEL: *020 7236 5650*

Above The Blackfriar, Blackfriars

FOUNDERS' ARMS

52 HOPTON STREET, SOUTHWARK, LONDON

This modern-looking pub on the south bank of the river next to Blackfriars bridge has possibly one of the best views over the impressive City skyline. St Paul's Cathedral stands tall in the foreground and the scales of justice of the Old Bailey, where some of the country's most notorious criminals have been tried and convicted, is visible in the background.

The pub also has some distinctive neighbours, including the old Bankside Power Station, now an extension of the main Tate Gallery in Pimlico, several miles upstream, and the Globe Theatre, a perfect example of how a building can be erected using the methods of hundreds of years ago.

The original Founders' Arms, sited near Founders' Wharf, was demolished in 1973. The present building was completed in 1979, though the pub had to wait 11 months for the roads and paths of the new Bankside Reach Development to be finished before it could begin serving the public.

The pub is at its most spectacular at night when its view of the City skyline is illuminated.

🕐 *11.00-11.00 Mon-Sat;*
12.00-10.30 Sun.
🍺 *Young's Bitter & Special, Young's seasonal beer. Cider: Strongbow.*
🍴 *12.00-2.30, 5.30-8.00 Mon-Fri; 12.30-8.00 Sat, Sun; 12.00-8.30 every day in summer.* Ⓥ
SYMBOLS: ❄ 🔳 🔳
TEL: *020 7928 1899*

Above Founders' Arms, Southwark

THE HORN TAVERN

29 KNIGHTRIDER STREET, LONDON, EC4

The Horn Tavern is one of the closest pubs on the north bank to the Millennium pedestrian bridge over the Thames. It was built by Christopher Wren, architect of St Paul's Cathedral and was a favoured haunt of Charles Dickens.

📷 *11.00-11.00 Mon-Fri; closed Sat, Sun.*
🍺 *Bass, Courage Best, occasional guest beer. Cider: Blackthorn.*
🍽 *12.00-2.30 Mon-Fri.* ⓥ
SYMBOLS: ❄ 🍴
TEL: *020 7236 1013*

ANCHOR

34 PARK STREET, BANKSIDE, LONDON

It is thought that there has probably been an inn on this site since the 15th century. It was from this pub that Samuel Pepys witnessed the Great Fire of London in 1666. The area surrounding this famous inn is a mixture of old and new, although these days the modern seems to predominate.

It has not always been such a respectable district: it was once notorious for its seediness and for being the haunt of rogues and vagabonds. Evidence has been found that bear- and bull-baiting pits were rife and the famous Clink (from where the phrase 'in the clink' originated) was one of five prisons in the area. Close by was Winchester Palace, the London home of the Bishop of Winchester, who also owned most of the surrounding land. The ladies of the night plying their services in the dark streets had to pay a percentage of their earnings to the Bishop. To satisfy his desires, he was waited upon by his own ladies, who became known as the Bishop of Winchester's Geese.

In 1876, the Anchor was destroyed by fire but it was soon replaced with the present building. One of the bars is named after Doctor Johnson, another regular at the pub and a close associate of Henry Thrale, who owned the then nearby, enormous Anchor Brewery. While Dr Johnson was a brilliant man who enjoyed good ale and fine food, he was not fond of washing. Once, while dining, a lady sitting next to him informed him that he smelt. He immediately replied 'you are mistaken madam. You smell, I stink.'

▦ *11.00-11.00 Mon-Sat; 12.00-10.30 Sun.*
▨ *Draught Bass, Flowers IPA, Greene King IPA, occasional guest beers. Cider: Strongbow.*
▥ *12.00-7.00 Mon-Sun.* Ⓥ
SYMBOLS: ❄ ♟ ▥ ⛄ ▣ ◪ *(planned)*
TEL: 020 *7407 1577*

207

THE BANKER

COUSIN LANE, LONDON, EC4

This no-frills drinking hole is hidden away beneath the arches of Cannon Street Railway Station, so you will hear the rumbling of trains overhead from time to time. Its viewing platform gives an excellent view of the fine stanchions of the bridge carrying the commuter trains across the river.

Like many City pubs it is closed at weekends, and it may also close early in the evening if trade is light, but it's worth seeking out for the sheer experience.

11.00-9.00 Mon-Fri; closed Sat, Sun.

Fuller's Chiswick Bitter, ESB & London Pride, Fuller's seasonal beer.
Cider: Strongbow.

12.00-3.00 Mon-Fri. (v)

SYMBOLS: ✳

TEL: *020 7283 5206*

OLD THAMESIDE INN
PICKFORDS WHARF, CLINK STREET, SOUTHWARK, LONDON

The old Pickford's Wharf warehouse, which at one time housed fine spices from around the world, has been tastefully refurbished and the Old Thameside Inn forms part of the new development. It has an excellent outside terrace overlooking the river and the dock of St Marie Overie, at present home to an exact replica of the Golden Hind, the original having disintegrated.

Mary Overy lived in London around the 10th century. Her father, John, operated the ferry across the river, a lucrative business that provided him with a good enough income to buy a considerable amount of property on the South Bank. A mean man, he decided to pretend to

be dead so that his family and friends would fast during their grief, thus saving money. Unfortunately, all those around him celebrated instead. Incensed with rage, he leapt out of bed, only to be killed by one of his servants who thought the devil had taken hold of him. Mary sent for her lover, who, while rushing to claim his inheritance, fell from his horse and broke his neck. The grief-stricken Mary used her father's money to fund a convent, into which she retired and rose to an elevated position because of her charitable works.

Inside this new hostelry there is a wealth of the exposed wooden beams and brickwork that formed part of the old warehouse, with large picture windows which oversee the river as well as the great metropolis.

🏠 *11.00-11.00 Mon-Fri; 12.00-6.00 Sat, Sun.*
🍺 *Adnams Best & Broadside, Marston's Pedigree, Tetley Bitter, regular guest beer. Cider: Blackthorn.*
🍴 *12.00-2.30 Mon-Fri; 12.00-4.00 Sat, Sun.* Ⓥ
SYMBOLS: ❄ 🏃 🏠 🔽
TEL: *020 7403 4243*

THE MARKET PORTER
9 STONEY STREET, LONDON, SE1

Sandwiched between the historic Borough Market and the less well-known Hop Exchange (now converted into offices) this mid-19th-century pub is only a stone's throw from the busy London Bridge Station. Original cobbled streets, curvaceous brick-built railway arches carrying the maze of railway lines to the south coast, and old riverside warehouses combine to provide an atmospheric setting of an age past.

If you fancy a drink in an old London boozer, the Market Porter is exactly what you have been looking for. The pub serves a mixed clientele of market traders, businessmen and tourists and, because of its location next to the market, the time-honoured licensing laws allow the pub to

open for business between 6.30 and 8.30 in the morning to serve those who have been grafting since the early hours. By all accounts it's one of the busiest times of day.

🗓 *6.30-8.30 am, 11.00-11.00 Mon-Sat; 12.00-10.30 Sun.*
🛢 *Courage Best, Fuller's London Pride, Harveys Sussex Best Bitter, 3 regular guest beers. Cider: Strongbow.*
🍽 *12.00-2.30 Mon-Sat.* Ⓥ
SYMBOLS: 🚹 🍽
TEL: *020 7407 2495*

Above The Market Porter, London, SE1

BARROWBOY & BANKER

BANK CHAMBERS, 6/8 BOROUGH HIGH STREET,
SOUTHWARK, LONDON

T his fine 19th-century building is on the approach to the new London Bridge. Formerly a bank, it closed in the mid-1990s and was converted into a pub, reopening in November 1996. Its close proximity to Borough Market, the oldest in London, explains the juxtaposition of cheeky barrowboy and serious banker in its name.

The grand frontage of Bank Chambers hides an even grander interior. As you enter through the towering wooden doors, you will be confronted by the most magnificent architecture: a high-beamed ceiling supported by marble columns, a majestic brass chandelier with arms sweeping out like flower buds, and a long winding bar with ornate upstand lights. A sweeping marble staircase, with carved wooden banisters that urge you to slide down them, leads to the open mezzanine floor that overlooks the resplendent hall. The wonderful wooden floors, antique prints, etched mirrors and large windows with long flowing curtains provide the finishing touches.

▥ *11.00-11.00 Mon-Fri; closed Sat, Sun.*
▦ *Fuller's Chiswick Bitter, ESB & London Pride, Fuller's seasonal beer. Cider: Scrumpy Jack.*
▦ *12.00-8.00 Mon-Fri.* Ⓥ
SYMBOLS: 👥
TEL: *020 7403 5415*

Right Barrowboy & Banker, Southwark

THE HUNG, DRAWN & QUARTERED
27 GREAT TOWER STREET, TOWER HILL, LONDON

The diarist Samuel Pepys wrote on the 13 October 1660: 'I went to see Major General Harrison hung, drawn & quartered. He was looking as cheerful as any man could in that condition.' Despite its name, taken from this historic and once common means of execution, the pub is very new. It opened its doors in 1996 following its conversion from bank premises and provides hospitality to those visiting

the nearby attractions including the famous Tower of London and the Monument to the Great Fire of London of 1666.

The cavernous interior, with a high ceiling supported by columns, was once where cashiers and other bank staff worked. High-backed wooden settles, antique prints and pictures, open wooden floors and atmospheric low-level lighting make this an enjoyable place to pass the time, in spite of the presence of the noose above the bar.

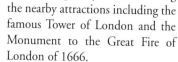

🕊 *11.00-11.00 Mon-Fri;*
12.00-3.00 Sat, Sun.
🍺 *Fuller's Chiswick Bitter, ESB &*
London Pride, Fuller's seasonal beer.
Cider: Scrumpy Jack.
🍴 *11.00 (12.00 Sun)-3.00*
Mon-Sun. Ⓥ
SYMBOLS: ✳
TEL: *020 7626 6123*

Above The Hung, Drawn & Quartered, Tower Hill

TOWER BRIDGE
TO
THE THAMES
BARRIER
(SOUTH SIDE OF THE RIVER)

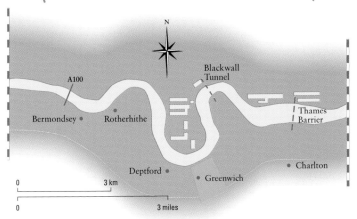

Once past Tower Bridge, the river starts the final stage of its
journey to the North Sea, ever widening, ever changing, ever
flowing. There are no more bridges during the rest of this
journey and you have to go underground to cross the river.

The embankment – once lined with docks, wharves and warehouses for trades associated with the river – is undergoing a major transformation and is fast becoming home to a vast number of offices and residential dwellings. Some of the old wharf buildings have been tastefully renovated and there are still areas where the old cobbled streets remain intact. Bermondsey is one such place and the old narrow streets and buildings give us a glimpse of the past. Jacob's Island in times gone by used to be a shelter for some of London's most notorious villains.

Rotherhithe, once known as Redriffe, is perhaps best known for its road-tunnel under the river. This village has a history of sailing ships and sailors, and it is from here that the Pilgrim Fathers set sail on the the *Mayflower* en route to Plymouth before its journey across the Atlantic Ocean to the New World.

As with so many of the riverside docks in this part of London, they are now redundant, no longer needed as they were in the days when countless ships brought in goods from all over the world. The Surrey Docks have suffered the same fate and now consist of houses and shops built around the old quaysides.

Deptford has remained largely untouched by the developers, mainly because most of the river front is taken up by the old Royal Naval Dockyard, which originated in 1573. Sir Francis Drake was knighted by Elizabeth I on board the *Golden Hind* here. The Royal Navy is no longer in residence and a number of commercial companies now operate from the yard. The Royal Navy Victualling Yard was also in Deptford, before the site became the Pepys Housing Estate, named after the great diarist who visited the area regularly.

Next comes one of the best-known places on the Thames – Greenwich, famous for so many things that it is difficult to know where to begin. A good starting point is Goddard's Pie & Mash shop, in existence since the late 19th century and the place to sample one of London's traditional meals of pie, mash and liquor. Unfortunately it no longer serves the marvellous delicacy of hot eels but the shop is hoping to reintroduce them in the future. Greenwich is famous for its association with the Navy and other aspects of life on the ocean wave. It is home to the giant tea-clipper *Cutty Sark*, which broke many records on its voyages to and from Australia by means of its 7,000 yards of canvas sail. The *Gipsy Moth IV*, in which Sir Francis Chichester sailed single-handedly round the world in 1966-7, is on display nearby.

The Royal Naval College started life as a royal palace for Charles II on the former site of the Palace of Placentia, a residence used by Henry VIII. He married Catherine of Aragon and Anne of Cleves in the Palace; his two daughters, Mary and Elizabeth, were born there; and it was where his son Edward VI died at the age of 16. The new building was used by royalty until William and Mary came to the throne, when it became a hospital for seamen. It served this purpose until 1873, then became a college.

The 3½ miles of galleries at the National Maritime Museum house many exhibits to Great Britain's naval history, including the uniform that Nelson wore at the Battle of Trafalgar. Queens House, built in 1618 in the classic Palladian style by Inigo Jones for Queen Anne of Denmark, now forms part of this great exhibition.

At the top of the hill in Greenwich Park is the Old Royal Observatory overlooking Greenwich and the rest of London. This 17th-century building still houses the time ball which when it was introduced in 1833 provided the first ever time signal for the ships on the river and the general public. It still drops at 13.00 local time every day. The Observatory marks the Prime Meridian line of Greenwich, which is used as a basis for time-keeping all over the world.

Down by the river front is a pedestrian tunnel linking Greenwich with the Isle of Dogs. It was built in 1902 in the face of much opposition from the many lightermen and watermen working the river who feared for their jobs.

Having passed the Royal Naval College, the river changes identity and along the embankment are many industrial companies that require access to the ships bringing in raw materials and taking out finished goods. Nearby is the underground Thames crossing, the Blackwall Tunnel, built in 1897. A second tunnel was added to it in 1967 to provide a separate carriageway for each direction of traffic.

On the North Greenwich Peninsula is the site of Millennium Experience, otherwise known as the Dome. It was built to house an impressive exhibition to celebrate the Millennium. It has a diameter of 320m, is 50m high, and twelve 100m steel masts support the largest domed structure in the world. A walk round the outside will take some time as it has a circumference of 1km with a floor area of 80,000 square metres.

Leaving the Millennium Village, the river passes Charlton and reaches the conclusion of our journey, the Thames Barrier. Based on the principle of a simple gas-cock, the eight giant metal-clad piers house the machinery to raise the mammoth gates that protect the inhabitants of London from high surge tides. It took eight years to build and was officially opened in 1984. Beyond this, there are no obstructions to those whose final destination is the sea.

Right Trafalgar Tavern, Greenwich

218

OLD JUSTICE

94 BERMONDSEY WALL EAST, BERMONDSEY, LONDON

This friendly community pub lies hidden away in the backstreets of Bermondsey. Another inn, the Old Justice in the Mint, once stood on the same site and, according to legend, was a sanctuary for debtors and villains seeking a safe haven from their pursuers. The pub was rebuilt in 1929, in what was then an area where industries such as brewing and tanning thrived. It had its moment of glory in 1984 when it was used in Paul McCartney's film *Give My Regards to Broadway*. The late Sir Ralph Richardson played the landlord.

Unusually, no food or cask-conditioned beers are served here, but don't let this deter you from visiting a classic pub.

🔲 *12.00-11.00 Mon-Sat; 12.00-4.00, 7.00-10.30 Sun.*
🔲 *Cider: Strongbow.*
SYMBOLS: ❄️ 👥 🔲 🍴
TEL: *020 7237 3452*

THE ANGEL

101 BERMONDSEY WALL EAST, ROTHERHITHE, LONDON

The art of providing good ale as well as rest for travellers was practised here in the 15th century when monks of Bermondsey Priory established a guesthouse. To reflect their religious beliefs, the inn was known as the Salutation, but became the Angell, following the Reformation, after the local lord of the manor, William Angell.

Its position by the river and closeness to the City of London has attracted some well-known visitors over the years. Diarist Samuel Pepys was a regular visitor – his mistress, the merry Mrs Bagwell, lived close by. He used to buy cherries from a Rotherhithe garden to take home to his wife, perhaps to allay any suspicions about his presence in the area. The explorer Captain James Cook is reputed to have stayed here before setting off on his voyage that would take him to Australia and New

Zealand. One other person who is said to have been a regular visitor was the infamous Judge Jeffreys who used to sit here and watch the action at Execution Dock on the other side of the river.

The present galleried inn was erected in the 1850s and provides a wonderful view of the Thames and the last London crossing over the river – Tower Bridge. Now standing alone in a prime position on the embankment, this inn, once the haunt of smugglers and pirates, is the ideal venue to sample some traditional delights of the area such as cockles and mussels.

🔳 *11.30-11.00 Mon-Sat; 12.00-10.30 Sun.*

🏛 *Thomas Greenall's Original, Worthington Best, occasional guest beer. Cider: Strongbow.*

🍴 *12.00-1.45 Mon-Fri, 7.00-9.30 Mon-Sat; 12.30-2.30 Sun.* Ⓥ

SYMBOLS: 🅿 ❄ 👫 🔳

TEL: *020 7237 3608*

THE SHIP
39/47 ST MARYCHURCH STREET, ROTHERHITHE, LONDON

As you would expect in an area so strongly associated with the river, there has been an abundance of pubs called the Ship. In 1825 there were four listed in Rotherhithe alone.

At one time this inn took a second name: the Great Eastern, perhaps to distinguish it from the others. The famous *Great Eastern* steamship was built by Isambard Kingdom Brunel at Burrells Wharf on the Isle of Dogs, so the name would have been very appropriate. At the time, this would have provided much employment in the area with some of the labour force coming from Rotherhithe. When the Wandsworth brewery Young's took over the pub in 1985 from Taylor Walker, it reverted to using its original name.

It's a wonderful backstreet community pub where some of the older locals will tell you about life here when the docks were in full flow.

11.00-11.00 Mon-Sat; 12.00-10.30 Sun.
Young's Bitter & Special. Cider: Blackthorn.
12.00-2.30 Mon-Sun. Ⓥ
SYMBOLS: ❄ 🏠 🐕 🏠
TEL: *020 7237 4103*

THE MAYFLOWER

117 ROTHERHITHE STREET, ROTHERHITHE, LONDON

In 1620 the Pilgrim Fathers set sail from Rotherhithe to Plymouth, and from there on their long journey to the New World. In charge of their ship, the *Mayflower*, was Captain Christopher Jones, with a crew of mainly local men. Their voyage started from this pub, then called the Shippe, built by the riverside in 1550. After delivering the Pilgrims safely to new shores, Captain Jones returned in the *Mayflower* to England in 1621, but he died a year later. His body lies in the graveyard of the local church of St Mary's.

The Shippe was rebuilt in the 18th century using wooden beams taken from the *Mayflower*. It was renamed the Spread Eagle & Crown and kept this title for over two hundred years until the pub was altered in the 1960s to resemble the original layout and finally redesignated as the Mayflower.

Don't be surprised if someone next to you at the bar asks for a first-class stamp; this historic inn is licensed to sell both English and American postage stamps. There's a jetty still in place outside, though the timbers seem too young to be the originals. The dark, dimly lit and cosy interior provides a wonderful drinking area which captures the spirit of the past.

🕐 *12.00-11.00 Mon-Sat; 12.00-10.30 Sun.*
🍺 *Greene King Abbot & IPA, Greene King seasonal beer.*
Cider: Strongbow.
🍴 *12.00-9.00 Mon-Sun.* Ⓥ
SYMBOLS: ❄ 👫 ⛵
TEL: *020 7237 4088*

The Blacksmith's Arms
257 ROTHERHITHE STREET, ROTHERHITHE, LONDON

The Blacksmith's Arms stands on the site where the guns were forged for the warships built at the nearby Deptford Naval Dockyard, which closed in 1869. The pub's half-timbered mock-Tudor front was added when the pub was rebuilt and extended in 1930.

Once very much a haunt of the local dockers, it still retains the old heated foot-rail where they could dry off their boots. The dockers used to play Down the Slot, a skilful game involving trying to drop ha'pennies through a hole in the floor. Bets would be placed on who could drop the most and all proceeds would be presented to the local hospital. A brass plate in the floor of the back room marks where the game was played. Players trying their luck these days have to use two pence coins. A marker on the bar shows the height the river rose to during the great flood of 1928 – more than six feet above the level predicted.

One customer has been drinking here for over sixty-four years, having first visited at the age of 16, before he joined the navy. He was present when HRH Queen Elizabeth the Queen Mother called in for a drink in 1998 when visiting the area.

When calling on this excellent pub, why not take time to look at the old black and white prints of how the area used to be and imagine the singsongs that used to take place round the piano that still sits in the bar.

12.00-11.00 Mon-Sat; 12.00-10.30 Sun.
Adnams Bitter, Fuller's ESB & London Pride, Fuller's seasonal beer.
Cider: Scrumpy Jack, Strongbow.
6.00-10.00 Mon-Sun. Ⓥ *(No food lunchtimes.)*
SYMBOLS: ❄ ⛹ ⛹ ⛹
TEL: *020 7237 1349*

THE DOG & BELL
116 PRINCE STREET, DEPTFORD, LONDON

I t is not possible to walk along the river at Deptford because of the old naval dockyards, now home to a number of commercial companies. The Thames Path takes a diversion round the backstreets and leads you to this perfect example of a traditional pub.

The three-storey Victorian building dating from 1849 was at one stage an alehouse where dock workers would congregate after a hard day's work. The dockyard, established by Henry VIII in 1573, was responsible for the building of many warships over the years but, because of silting up of the Thames and the lowering of ships' hulls, it was no longer possible to launch them from here so the yard closed in 1869. Two years later it reopened as a cattle market and continued in that role until 1913.

The name is thought to refer to the time when there was a lot of marshland surrounding the river here. The hunters would first ring a bell to scare the birds into the air, then, after shooting them, let their dogs loose to retrieve them.

The Dog & Bell has had a listing in the Campaign for Real Ale's *Good Beer Guide* for more than 15 years. The pub not only serves superb-quality cask-conditioned ales at reasonable prices: the food takes some beating too.

🎵 *11.00-11.00 Mon-Sat; 12.00-10.30 Sun.*
🍺 *Fuller's ESB & London Pride, 3 regular guest beers. Cider: Stowford Press.*
🍽 *12.00-2.30 Mon-Sun.* ⓥ
SYMBOLS: ❄ 🎵 🍽 🍴
TEL: *020 8692 5664*

THE GIPSY MOTH
60 GREENWICH CHURCH STREET, GREENWICH, LONDON

There has been a public house on this site, in one of the busiest parts of Greenwich, since 1795 though until 1973 it was called the Wheatsheaf. The pub is now named after the boat used by Sir Francis Chichester when he single-handedly circumnavigated the globe in 1966-7, the first person in the world to do this. He was knighted at Greenwich by the Queen, who used the same sword that Elizabeth I had used to knight Sir Francis Drake when he landed the *Golden Hind* at Deptford following his second voyage around the world. *Gipsy Moth IV* now rests in dry dock overlooking the river in the shadow of the mighty *Cutty Sark*.

Within the pub are souvenirs, maps and artefacts relating to the great voyage taken by the second Sir Francis. It's a large busy pub, and caters for the many visitors to this historic village from all round the world.

🕒 *11.00-11.00 Mon-Sat; 12.00-10.30 Sun.*

🍺 *Adnams Best, Morland Old Speckled Hen, Tetley Bitter, occasional guest beer. Cider: Blackthorn.*

🍴 *12.00-3.00 Mon-Sun.* Ⓥ *(No food evenings.)*

SYMBOLS: 🦮 🚻 🏨

TEL: *020 8858 0786*

TRAFALGAR TAVERN
PARK ROW, GREENWICH, LONDON

Viscount Horatio Nelson, the English naval commander, fought bravely at the Battle of Trafalgar in 1805 and achieved a great victory for his country over the French and Spanish fleets, but he paid the ultimate price for this – his life. When his body was returned to Greenwich by boat the entourage passed an inn called the Old George, which had been there since the early 1700s. When this was demolished, a magnificent new building designed by the surveyor at the local Greenwich Hospital was built. When it opened in 1837, the year that Queen Victoria succeeded to the throne, it was called the Trafalgar Tavern, a salute to the great seafarer.

With the river so close, it is perhaps not surprising that fish was a main feature on the menu. Diners were able to sample delicacies such as spitchcocked eels, stewed carp, even lobster omelette; but it was whitebait (small young herrings, sprats or other similar fish) that were to bring it such fame that the pub attracted great politicians such as William Pitt and Gladstone. The Whitebait Dinners of cabinet ministers then became a regular outing.

Other users of this majestic tavern were Charles Dickens, William Thackeray, Doctor Johnson, Doctor Crippen and, reputedly, Dick

Turpin – who seems to have spent so much of his time in various inns across the country that it's hard to believe he had time to carry out his wicked deeds. In his *Dictionary of the Thames*, the younger son of Charles Dickens, also named Charles, wrote: 'There is no next morning headache like that which follows a Greenwich dinner.'

The tavern closed for business in 1915 and became an institution for old seamen, then a working men's club. Plans to demolish it altogether were made in the 1930s, but these were scuppered by the Second World

War. It stayed closed until 1965, when it was exquisitely refurbished, then reopened to the public.

This grand building in its prime location next to the Thames provides the perfect venue to sample the delights of whitebait, which is still served to this day.

🍴 *11.30-11.00 Mon-Sat; 12.00-10.30 Sun.*

🍺 *Courage Best & Directors, Morland Old Speckled Hen, regular Flagship Brewery guest beers. Cider: Scrumpy Jack.*

🍽 *12.00-10.00 Tues-Sat; 12.00-3.00 Sun, Mon.* Ⓥ

SYMBOLS: 🚹 🏠 🖼 🡆

TEL: *020 8858 2437*

THE YACHT

5-7 CRANE STREET, GREENWICH, LONDON

An inn has stood on this site for longer than any other in Greenwich. In fact, Crane Street is one of the oldest thoroughfares in the village though traffic is not a problem as the road is too narrow to allow access to any motor traffic. The Prime Meridian, or zero line of longitude as it is sometimes known, runs right through this riverside inn.

During the Second World War, the building was partially destroyed by an enemy bomb.

The small frontage is deceiving, as you will realise once you have stepped inside. The raised area overlooking the river is the best place to sample the house fish and chips, made using a secret recipe beer batter.

🍴 *11.00-11.00 Mon-Sat; 12.00-10.30 Sun.*

🍺 *Theakston's Best & XB, regular guest beer. Cider: Scrumpy Jack.*

🍽 *as pub opening hours.* Ⓥ

SYMBOLS: ❄ 🚹 🍺

TEL: *020 8858 0175*

CUTTY SARK
BALLAST QUAY, LASSELL STREET, GREENWICH, LONDON

It's difficult to miss this old inn from the river: its name is spelled out in large letters painted on the large Georgian bow window with curved sashes. If you're travelling by car or foot it's a bit more difficult to find, but certainly worth the effort.

Reputedly built in 1805 or earlier according to some, it replaced a pub called the Green Man. It was known as the Union Tavern until 1954 when the name was changed to coincide with the arrival of the great tea clipper to the dry dock at Greenwich.

Ballast Quay, where at one time ships would load with Blackheath gravel to act as ballast for their return voyages to their homelands, has all the makings of a period setting – cobbled streets, old terraced houses with front doors leading directly on to the pavement, and the grand harbourmaster's office built in 1840.

The interior of the inn is far removed from the 20th century. There are flagstone floors, tables and chairs made from old barrels, and a grand fireplace. The regal wooden staircase rises to the first floor gallery with a multitude of rooms in all directions.

The stupendous riverside terrace is one of the last stopping places before the cityscape changes to a scene of industrialisation.

🔲 *11.00-11.00 Mon-Sat; 12.00-10.30 Sun.*
🍺 *Bass, Fuller's London Pride, Morland Old Speckled Hen, Young's Special, occasional guest beer. Cider: Blackthorn.*
🍴 *11.00-9.00 Mon-Sat; 12.00-9.00 Sun.* Ⓥ
SYMBOLS: ❄ 👫 🔲 🔲
TEL: *020 8858 3146*

Above Cutty Sark, Greenwich

THE PILOT INN
68 RIVER WAY, GREENWICH, LONDON

The Pilot started life as a small alehouse in 1801 when this was a busy industrial area. It catered for the watermen working on the river, who would rest on the wooden settles in the small bar, spinning yarns about what they had seen on the river that day. During the 19th century, a terrace of cottages known as Ceylon Place were built next door. Over the years, the area went downhill and the pub became a no-frills meeting place for the working man. The decline continued until the area became virtually derelict and eventually the brewers threw in the towel, placing the pub on the market in 1984.

It was purchased at a very low price by a local family, who then set about with grim determination to change the pub into somewhere everyone would enjoy visiting. The icing was put on the cake when the news broke of the redevelopment of the nearby North Greenwich Peninsula, and the construction on the site of the Millennium Dome, or Millennium Experience.

🕙 *11.00-11.00 Mon-Sat;*
12.00-10.30 Sun.
🍺 *Courage Best, Fuller's London*
Pride, Young's Special.
Cider: Blackthorn.
🍽 *12.00-2.30 Mon-Sat; 6.00-*
9.00 Mon-Fri, 6.30-10.00 Sat;
12.00-4.30 Sun. Ⓥ
SYMBOLS: 🅿 ❄ 🚻 🈁 ↩
TEL: *020 8858 5910*

Above The Pilot Inn, Greenwich

ANCHOR & HOPE
RIVERSIDE, CHARLTON, LONDON

An inn is thought to have been on this site since the 16th century, when it would have provided refreshment to the sailors who anchored their ships at nearby Vasey's Wharf, one of the oldest on the Thames. Here they would rest, hoping for a return trip across the seas.

The present riverside building was constructed in 1899, to a strange design with a turret and cupola and an open veranda on the first floor. During the Second World War, the pub was extensively damaged when a V1 flying bomb hit the United Glass Bottles works behind the pub. Thanks to the War Damage Act, it was rebuilt and reopened to the public.

A past landlady, one Mrs Sergeant, was often to be seen in the bar in her pinnie and with her hair in curlers. She served only the customers she liked: if she didn't like the look of you, you would not be allowed in.

The present, far more amenable, landlord worked on the river as a

lighterman for most of his life and was eventually made a Freeman of the River Thames. He has always lived in Charlton, within two miles of the pub.

Maps and charts of the river adorn the high-ceilinged open-plan bar. The outside seating area has a commanding view of the Thames Barrier, which will protect London from the onslaught of an unusually high tide.

🛏 *11.00-11.00 Mon-Sat; 12.00-10.30 Sun.*
🍺 *occasionally. Cider: Blackthorn.*
🍽 *12.00-4.00 Mon-Sun.* Ⓥ
Open from 10.00 am for breakfast.
SYMBOLS: ❄ 👬 🛏
TEL: *020 8858 0382*

TOWER BRIDGE
TO
THE THAMES
BARRIER
(NORTH SIDE OF THE RIVER)

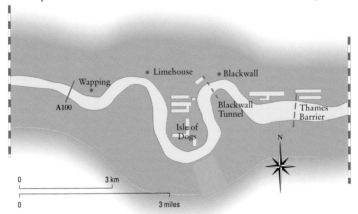

After Tower Bridge on the north side of the river, the first
landmark is St Katherine's Dock. Built in 1828 and designed by
the Scottish civil engineer Thomas Telford, the docks flourished
until they were badly damaged in the Second World War.

They were eventually closed to trade in 1968, but were not forgotten: this dock was the first of its kind to be restored and there are converted warehouses, shops, houses and a marina containing some fine examples of Thames sailing barges now on the site.

Wapping soon appears, and what a history this area has. Crooks, thieves, pirates, murderers and ladies of the night all congregated to make this one of the most unpleasant parts of town during the 16th and 17th centuries. At one stage there were 36 taverns in Wapping High Street and it was here, in the dark and dingy alehouses, that the undesirables met to plan their crimes. If caught, chances were they would end up in Execution Dock to be hanged, then tied to piles at low tide and left until three tides had washed over their bodies before being taken away.

The area has changed dramatically since then and the old warehouses and wharves have been converted into private residences, but not at the expense of the wonderful character of the area. A few of the old inns still remain to give you a reminder of the past.

Moving on, the north side of the Rotherhithe Tunnel emerges from its journey underground and marks the start of Limehouse, named for the old lime kilns that were in this area until 1935. It was also

Left The Barley Mow, Limehouse

known as Chinatown in the late-19th century because of its reputation for corruption and the dens of iniquity where opium was sold. Now the area has been cleaned up and consists mainly of quality housing. Limehouse Basin provides a link from the Thames to the River Lea and the Grand Union Canal, which at one time opened up routes from the Port of London to the rest of the country by means of the extensive internal canal system.

The river now takes a sharp turn south and begins its journey round the Isle of Dogs. No one is quite sure how it came to be called this, but one explanation is that this favourite hunting ground of Henry VIII was where he kennelled his dogs. Until the end of the 19th century the area still consisted of pastures and marshland but, because of major overcrowding problems at the Port of London, Parliament agreed to the building of new docks on the Isle of Dogs. The first to be built was the West India Docks, which opened in 1802, followed by the South West India Dock and finally Millwall Docks. For many, many years local dockers unloaded the cargoes of ships from far-flung corners of the globe, before they were distributed to other parts of the country.

With the advent of containerisation, the London docks laid dormant for many years until the birth of the London Docklands Development Corporation. When the builders moved in the whole area changed: new buildings sprang up around the old docks, which have been retained, creating a whole new working environment for the companies that had been attracted to the area by grants and cheap office accommodation. Canary Wharf, which at 800 feet high is the tallest building in the United Kingdom, now dominates the Isle of Dogs and can be seen from most parts of London. Between the perimeter road round the island and the river are more new developments of apartments and houses to transform the Thames embankment. Beyond the Isle, on the east side, is Blackwall where the second tunnel under the Thames originates.

From here to the north side of the Thames Barrier, industry takes over and dominates the riverside – a reminder of the past and present commercial importance of this mighty river.

TOWN OF RAMSGATE

62 WAPPING HIGH STREET, WAPPING, LONDON

The small, inconspicuous frontage of this famous pub gives no clue to its historic past. The first inn on the site, the Hostel, was built some time in the 1460s. During the 17th century, the name was changed to the Red Cow, supposedly after a pretty barmaid with distinctive red locks. At this time the Wapping area was a hive of activity and the Red Cow would have been a centre for swapping tales and spending hours of merriment for those who found themselves in this seedy part of London.

George Jeffreys, the hanging judge responsible for the demise of many rebels whom he tried, helped to put this old inn firmly on the map. When his ally King James II was forced to flee to France in 1688, Jeffreys knew that his position was threatened so he planned to escape the country. He made his way to Wapping where he secured a passage on a coal ship due to leave the next day. He disguised himself as a sailor and lay low in the Red Cow until his ship was ready to sail. Unfortunately, he was recognised by a lawyer's clerk who informed the search party chasing the judge of his whereabouts. Jeffreys was seized in Wapping and carted off to face trial for his deeds. He was

subsequently imprisoned in the Tower of London, where he died of kidney disease at the age of 41.

Wapping Old Stairs, next to the pub, was at one time used by fishermen from Ramsgate to land their catches before they were taken to market. This explains how the name Town of Ramsgate came to be in the hat when a new name was being chosen for the pub in the 19th century.

The interior is long and narrow, dark yet with a bright atmosphere, smoky ceilings and plentiful wood panelling, which all combine to make this a memorable place to visit.

🕐 *11.00-11.00 Mon-Sat; 12.00-10.30 Sun.*
🍺 *Draught Bass, Fuller's London Pride, regular guest beer. Cider: Blackthorn.*
🍴 *12.00-3.00, 6.00-8.00 Mon-Fri; 12.00-6.00 Sat; 12.00-4.00 Sun.* Ⓥ
SYMBOLS: ❄
TEL: *020 7264 0001*

CAPTAIN KIDD
108 WAPPING HIGH STREET, WAPPING, LONDON

There has been a pub on this site since only 1990, which might explain why its presence may not be immediately obvious. It is set in what used to be known as St John's Wharf, a dockland warehouse that for many years stored imported coffee and fruit. The pub was named after Captain William Kidd, a Scottish merchant seaman who was branded a pirate, arrested in the American colonies and eventually hanged at Execution Dock on 23 May 1701.

🕐 *11.00-11.00 Mon-Sat; 12.00-10.30 Sun.Cider: Samuel Smith.*
🍴 *12.00-3.00, 6.30-10.00 Mon-Sun.* Ⓥ *Light snacks only in bar. (Restaurant facilities available).*
SYMBOLS: ❄ 🚻 🏠
TEL: *020 7480 5759*

PROSPECT OF WHITBY
57 WAPPING WALL, WAPPING, LONDON

Sandwiched between two modern developments, this ancient inn dating back to 1520 claims to be one of the oldest in London. At one time, it was known as the Devil's Tavern, which gives some idea as to its customers. However, in 1777, the name was changed to the Prospect of Whitby, apparently after a square-rigger that carried coal from the Tyne to London and called at the pub en route.

Judge Jeffreys lived nearby in the aptly named Butchers Row and used to stop here on his way to and from Execution Dock. Other notables who frequented this tavern over the years were Charles Dickens, Dr Johnson, J.M.W. Turner, and Samuel Pepys.

In 1780, a sailor called John Westcombe was accredited with introducing the fuschia into this country. On his return from afar, he sold the shrub to a market gardener for a noggin of rum.

In 1953 a certain Captain John Cunningham was hosting a function in the pub. During the evening a gang of thieves led by Robert Harrington-Saunders (better known as Scarface) invited the guests to hand over their valuables, then they fled. Saunders was caught, but he murdered one of his pursuers and was sentenced to life imprisonment.

Though the surrounding area has changed much over the years, the interior of the pub is a monument to its past: old beer barrels support a pewter counter (which some unfortunate person has to clean every day) worn flagstone floors, gas lamps and wood galore all blend happily together. A wooden veranda overlooking the river completes the scene.

🕒 *11.30-3.00, 5.30-11.00 Mon-Fri; 11.30-11.00 Sat; 12.00-10.30 Sun.*

🍺 *Courage Best & Directors, Marston's Pedigree, occasional guest beer. Cider: Strongbow.*

🍴 *12.00-2.30 Mon-Sat, 12.00-3.00 Sun; 6.00-9.00 Mon-Sun.* Ⓥ

SYMBOLS: ❄ 🚹 🚾 ♨ ✈

TEL: *020 7481 1095*

Above Prospect of Whitby, Wapping

THE BARLEY MOW

44 NARROW STREET, LIMEHOUSE, LONDON

This colourful Edwardian building, which was erected in 1905, housed the dockmaster of Limehouse Basin when this part of the river was alive with docks and industry. Now this has all disappeared and the former dockmaster's residence was converted into a pub in 1989.

Its name is not associated with farming, but comes from the Barley Mow brewery that was close by. The brewery was opened in 1730 by the London company Taylor Walker. The area along the river became known as Brewery Wharf. Here ale was brewed, then stored in wooden barrels before its journey to pubs and other outlets all over the world. The company of Taylor Walker flourished and became one of London's finest brewers, opening a new brewery in Limehouse in 1889. It remained in operation until 1960, when the company merged with Ind Coope and the brewery closed for good.

The pub's large riverside terrace and its elevated position by the entrance to Limehouse Basin allows an excellent panoramic view of the river, though the volume of traffic has now subsided and only a handful of passenger and other craft pass by or enter Limehouse Basin.

▥ *12.00-11.00 Mon-Sat; 12.00-10.30 Sun.*
▣ *Burton Ale, Marston's Pedigree Tetley Bitter. Cider: Blackthorn.*
⑩ *12.00-2.30 Mon-Fri, 12.00-3.00 Sat, Sun;*
6.30-10.00 Mon-Sat, 6.30-9.00 Sun. ⓥ
SYMBOLS: 🅿 ❄ 🚻 ▥
TEL: *020 7265 8931*

THE GRAPES
76 NARROW STREET, LIMEHOUSE, LONDON

There's always been some debate about whether this inn was the model for that in Dickens' *Our Mutual Friend*, or whether the honour should go to the Two Brewers which used to be at Dukes Shore in Limehouse. Whichever it was, this pub of pubs stands on its own merit, not needing any literary support.

Its history can be traced back to 1604 when a 500-year lease on the premises was granted to a John Bigott. It was another hundred years before any reference was made to the house being used for the sale of alcohol. Unfortunately, about 15 years later it and the neighbouring houses were burned down. The present grand four-storey brick structure was built on the site by John Stonehaur.

At one time in its dark and dingy past, getting drunk in the Grapes was not recommended because it was not uncommon for totally inebriated customers to be taken by boat out into the middle of the river and drowned. The body would then be sold for dissection to doctors who didn't seem to care where the subjects came from. All they were

interested in was a constant supply of fresh corpses on which they could work to further their studies.

The exterior of the Grapes is impressive, with a small frontage and etched glass windows, but the long and narrow interior is even more exciting. The bare floorboards and old tables, chairs and settles of every description blend with the local artefacts to produce a spectacular show. The crowning glory is the wooden veranda overlooking the river where it is possible at high tide to lean out and feel the waters of the Thames. The pub is famed for the fish dishes, and you can eat in the informal downstairs bar or, for something special, in the first floor restaurant.

🕛 *12.00-3.00, 5.30-11.00 Mon-Fri; 7.00pm -11.00pm Sat, 12.00-3.00, 7.00-10.30 Sun. (Not open Sat lunchtimes.)*

🍺 *Adnams Best, Burton Ale, regular guest beer.*

🍴 *12.00-2.00 Mon-Fri, 12.00-3.00 Sun; 7.00-9.00 Mon-Sun.* Ⓥ

SYMBOLS: ❄ 🍽

TEL: *020 7987 4396*

Above The Grapes, Limehouse

City Pride

15 WEST FERRY ROAD, ISLE OF DOGS, LONDON

I n the last 15 years all the wharves, ships, cranes, old warehouses, dockers' houses – in fact virtually everything to do with the old docks – have gone from the Isle of Dogs, to be replaced with office blocks and the giant Canary Wharf towering above all of east London.

The City Pride was built some time in the early 20th century when the docks would have been at their peak. A large pub, it sits between the old West Ferry Road and the new Marsh Wall, with the front and back entrances swapped to suit the new road layout.

Its internal transformation from working men's pub to something

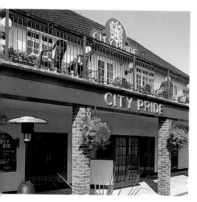

more upmarket has changed the customers from river workers to the white-collar staff from the many companies that have left the City to move to the new Docklands development. An excellent point from which to watch the annual London Marathon.

🕐 *12.00-11.00 Mon-Sat; 12.00-10.30 Sun.*
🍺 *Tetley Bitter. Cider: Blackthorn.*
🍴 *12.00-3.00, 6.00-10.00 Mon-Fri; 12.00-4.00, 5.00-8.00 Sat, Sun.* Ⓥ
SYMBOLS: 🅿 ❀
TEL: *020 7987 3516*

The Ferry House

26 FERRY STREET, ISLE OF DOGS, LONDON

A n inn has stood on this site since Tudor times. Along with a chapel, they were at one stage the only buildings on the island. When Secretary to the Admiralty, Samuel Pepys used a ferry at this point of the river when going about his official naval business.

Apparently he once said: 'I used to like standing at the Ferry House, whilst waiting for the ferry from the Isle to Greenwich, because I could always put my hand up the barmaid's skirt and she wouldn't scream.'

In 1822, the present building was erected by order of the Greenwich Ferry Society to house the ferryman. Between the raising and lowering of the flag to indicate the arrival and departure of the ferry, his wife would sell beer to the waiting customers. The ferry service continued until the Greenwich foot tunnel opened in 1902 by which time the area was a hive of activity, mainly associated with the river and shipping.

Now the industry has gone to be replaced by luxurious riverside apartments, but the heritage of this traditional back street pub carries on.

11.00-11.00 Mon-Sat; 12.00-10.30 Sun.

Courage Best & Directors, Tetley Bitter. Cider: Strongbow.

11.00-2.30 Mon-Sun. Ⓥ

SYMBOLS: 🚹 🐕 🍺

TEL: *020 7987 5141*

THE WATERMANS ARMS
1 GLENAFFRIC AVENUE, MILLWALL, LONDON

This was once a famous East End pub called the Newcastle Arms. The 1960s television personality Dan Farsen took over the tenancy in 1962 and his presence attracted many famous stars to the pub, including Judy Garland who sang in the road under a streetlight when her manager wouldn't let her perform inside.

Now very different from its heyday.

11.00-11.00 Mon-Sat; 12.00-10.30 Sun.
Watermans Bitter. Cider: Blackthorn.
12.00-3.00, 5.00-8.00 Mon-Sun. Ⓥ
SYMBOLS: ❄ 🕴 🏠
TEL: *020 7538 0712*

THE PIER TAVERN
299 MANCHESTER ROAD, ISLE OF DOGS, LONDON

In an area where pubs have come and gone, only the fittest survive, the friendly Pier Tavern being one of these. The building was constructed during the early-19th century; it was totally refurbished in 1997 to adapt to the change of clientele that has occurred in the area.

While some pubs have a wealth of history, this one's past seems to have vanished without a trace. However, despite the changes, this traditional docklands pub has retained all the character you would expect..

11.00-11.00 Mon-Sat; 12.00-10.30 Sun.
Boddingtons Bitter, Fuller's London Pride, Wadworth 6X, occasional guest beer. Cider: Old Rosie, Strongbow.
12.00-3.00, 5.30-9.30 Mon-Fri; 12.00-9.30 Sat, Sun (V).
SYMBOLS: ❄ 🕴 🏠
TEL: *020 7515 9528*

THE QUEEN OF THE ISLE

571 MANCHESTER ROAD, ISLE OF
DOGS, LONDON

This old tavern advertises itself as being the friendliest pub on the island, but only a visit here will reveal the truth. It started life as the Queen's Hotel, but at some stage during its life, took on this new title. The sign depicts a picture of Britannia – a symbol of the greatness of Britain.

At one time, this triangular-shaped building, which resembles the bow of a ship, had five bars, but following a refurbishment in 1995, the interior was changed to a single drinking area.

11.00-11.00 Mon-Sat; 12.00-10.30 Sun.
Flowers IPA, Wadworth 6X, occasional guest beer. Cider: Scrumpy Jack.
12.00-5.00 Mon-Sun in winter; 12.00-9.00 Mon-Sun all other times of year. Ⓥ
SYMBOLS: ✳ ⛹ ⛴
TEL: *020 7537 3270*

THE GUN

27 COLDHARBOUR, BLACKWALL, LONDON

When the Henry Addington became the first ship to enter the West India Docks in 1802, a 21-gun salute was sounded to mark the occasion. This may be the reason for the inn's name, or it may be because of the old foundry called Gun Yard that used to be nearby.

There has been a hostelry on this site for over two hundred and fifty years; the name of the street, Coldharbour, is derived from an alehouse that provided only cold shelter (ie didn't serve hot food). Smugglers using the bar kept a watch for excise men out on the river through a spyhole in the wall by the spiral staircase at the rear of the pub.

It was here that Admiral Horatio Nelson would meet with his mistress Lady Hamilton while he was visiting the local foundries to inspect the guns being made for his fleet. It is said that Emma Hamilton waited for her lover in an upstairs room in the Gun, passing the time away by knitting.

It is a traditional pub with no airs and graces. As with many of the riverside pubs in this area, most of the trade used to come from the dockers and the men who earned their living from the river. It is still frequented by the seamen from the West India Docks, who have signed their ships flags, which are now hanging from the pub's ceiling.

11.00-11.00 Mon-Sat; 12.00-10.30 Sun.

Marston's Pedigree, Nelson House Bitter. Cider: Blackthorn, Strongbow.

12.00-2.30 Mon-Sun. Ⓥ

SYMBOLS: ❄ 👫 🏠 🍴

TEL: *020 7987 1692*

INDEX